Best Foot Forward

My Fight for Justice

Diane Taylor

ABOUT THE AUTHOR

Diane Taylor was born in Northern Ireland. The second eldest of five children, she achieved fame in the principality as a popular model in the 1990s. She has been an army wife, a hotel receptionist and a PA to an alarm company director. A fun, fit and fearless female, Diane is now a tireless campaigner for the rights of those who find themselves victims of institutional corruption.

Her biggest achievement has been as a home-maker and a doting mother to up-and-coming fellow model and businesswoman, her daughter Sophia. Her story has been featured in the Sunday World, where she was seen in her modelling days, and she has recently appeared in photo shoots with her daughter.

ACKNOWLEDGEMENTS

Thanks to :

Judge Philpot R.I.P

Jim Patterson (Podiatrist)

Mr Kilmartin (Podiatric Surgeon)

Janice Reid (Care Expert)

for their truth and integrity.

Alex Easton for his continued steadfast support over the last several years.

Alex Gerrains (RIP)

Terry Mullins

Marty mc Gartland

Danny (my brother)

John Magil

David Walker

Dave Loyd

Dedicated to Sophia, my daughter, and Kevin, my partner.

D Taylon

Prologue

The Changeling

This was a very powerful movie. I recall watching it when I was in the middle of my particular nightmare. Angelina Jolie played the part wonderfully as the single parent, Christine Collins. Returning home late from work one Saturday night, she finds her nine-year-old son, Walter, has disappeared off the face of the earth. The police arrive but it's a complete mystery and we are led to believe the boys in blue from the Los Angeles Police Department (LAPD) are perhaps just a little too relaxed about the boy's disappearance. He's just another runaway on their books, not altogether uncommon, especially when it's the son of a single parent without the discipline and influence of a father figure to keep the boy in check.

We see the effect on the protagonist in the weeks and months following her son's disappearance. We are also left wondering if she is heading towards a breakdown as she tells the police on more than one occasion that she feels they are not doing enough. The local pastor also gets involved in a campaign vilifying the LAPD citing incompetence, corruption and sheer laziness. Eventually, the police announce that they have found her boy but, when they are reunited, she realises they have returned a total stranger to her. It is a charade with their lame effort to deflect the accusations of ineptitude. Her attempts to get justice had brought her into conflict with the LAPD who were prepared to go to any lengths to protect their reputation. All of a sudden, it's one girl against some very powerful people and when she continues to complain, she finds herself arrested.

I heard a noise and realised it was my heavy breathing as I wiped a bead of perspiration from my brow. Angelina's character almost mirrored my persona. Her treatment at the hands of those in authority was almost identical to mine. I watched the screen with my hand over my mouth. I thought to myself – No! Can't they see she's telling the truth? I knew what was coming next. Eventually, they confined her to a mental ward.

We might think - How can that happen?

My memories took me back to being 18 years of age when I was sectioned in a mental hospital for a short period. My time in hospital was horrendous. It holds horrific memories. I knew I didn't belong there. Thankfully I didn't have to worry for too long as I only spent two days in the hospital before my father and my uncle Alex, who was a priest, got involved and I was released. I couldn't have imagined staying there a day longer and was more than aware that the atmosphere and the other patients were sucking the life out of me.

Several years later I discovered that The Changeling was based on a true story. The Wineville Chicken Coop Murders were a series of abductions and murders of young boys between 1926 and 1928 by Gordon Northcott who sexually abused the youngsters, kept them in a chicken coop for his gratification and eventually murdered them. Although they never found young Walter's body, it is believed he was one of Northcott's victims.

My own story does not feature any child sexual abuse or murder … nothing quite as dramatic as that. What makes my story worse is that the hell I went through was the result of nothing more than a minor neighbourhood dispute. The neighbour I chose to disagree with had friends and family in high places, she made it her number one priority to ruin my life and break me.

This is my story.

Part One

1

The Early Days, Moulding my Character

I was the second eldest of five siblings. My sister Ruth came first, then me, followed by Debbie and next Tanya, all of us within a year of each other. My parents never thought they would end up with a boy but my brother, Danny Jr, came along much, much later. He was the spoiled one of the family, but for all that, he was my favourite. I guess it was my maternal instincts coming through right from the start.

My brother and I were very close. As for us four girls, we thought nothing of pulling each other's hair out while wrestling one another to the ground. Our little cat-fights brought constant despair to our poor mother, Mavis. There was one thing that set me apart from my sisters. It clicked one day as I heard one of our neighbours joking with mum, 'Is Diane the coalman's or the milkman's?' she said. All of my siblings were blonde-haired and, although I loved my long black hair, it set me apart from the rest.

My poor, over-sensitive mother would take offence to these cacklings and, more often than not, would leave me at home with my father. He was a self-employed painter and decorator and I was definitely *Daddy's girl* way back then. We bonded closely as he often took me to the hospital for tests because I had been born with a heart murmur. This was something else that set me apart from my sisters and my brother. I knew I was different but I also felt special too. I loved staying at home with my dad. He had a heart of gold and would have done anything for anyone.

For people who wonder where I get my spark from, my dad had a fiery temper and was outspoken on a whole gamut of subjects. He always said it as he saw it and there was never any holding back. I learned about his temperament by watching him from as early as I can remember. He taught me how to fight my corner and told me that if I believed something was just then it was always worth fighting for.

We lived in the small town of Larne, a seaport on the east coast of County Antrim, Northern Ireland. As the history books will tell you, there was a lot of trouble going on in the 1970s. Although there had been disharmony in Northern Ireland for centuries, the *Troubles*, as they were known, had been worsening since the August riots in 1969 and night-time curfews were put in place in Catholic areas such as the Falls Road in Belfast. In 1972 all hell broke loose when British troops shot and killed 13 unarmed civilians at an anti-internment rally in Derry on 30 January. It sent shock waves around the world and, overnight, the place I called home had changed.

We moved to a predominantly Protestant area of Carrickfergus in the early 1980s. All the family on my mother's side were of that persuasion and my father's side Catholic. Having this polarity makes you realise that, in the end, these are just labels. People are people, regardless of their religion, race or creed. Every side has their good eggs and bad eggs, and there's no faction which can classify itself as being perfect.

Not that this stopped others making a big issue of our Catholicism. As children, we hated the place where we now found ourselves. It seemed like we were the only Catholics there, and were called *fenian bastards* by people of all ages, often being spat upon. How these hypocrites would think kids as young as us would know anything about centuries of a revolutionary nationalist organisation is still beyond me. It was a miserable few years for us, but eventually, we moved to a nicer, more balanced area in Carrickfergus. I went to a comprehensive secondary school, again making me different from the rest of my siblings as most of them went to the grammar school. It seemed that I was going to remain cast as the rebellious black sheep, matching my hair colour!

I was in fourth year of school when I was victim to a horrendous beating. This was dealt out by a girl who was supposed to be my sister's friend. We had bumped into each other in the cloak room at break time and she was in a furious mood. 'Watch where you're fucking walking!' she shouted at me.

I replied in all innocence, 'It's you who banged into me.'

I thought nothing of it and a few minutes later I walked into the girls' toilets where she was washing her hands. She looked up, gave me a dirty look and, before I knew it, she had launched herself at me and attacked me with her nails. There were no punches thrown but I became aware of what she was trying to do and did my best to cover my face. My sister told me this girl had deliberately sharpened her nails at break time with a nail file. She was in the year above me, bigger, more powerful and determined to leave her mark on my face. She left me on the toilet floor in a pool of blood. Mission accomplished for her. These wounds were not just emotionally damaging, as the attack left me with several facial scars for years.

My mum and dad were not happy about this, to say the least. When I arrived home, it looked like I had been attacked by a wild animal. The very next day my mother and father demanded a meeting with one of the heads of the school and the school's priest. My parents left them in no doubt that they were going to sue the school over the incident as well as for the trauma and distress it had caused. Somehow, with considerable cajoling and implied threats coming the other way, they were talked out of doing so. Despite the mess my face had been left in, it was almost as if they denied the attack had ever taken place.

The following year, I was moved on. My parents decided to send me to a different school because of the attack and because talks had broken down with the head of the school and the school's priest. The new school was 14 miles away from my home. Living so far from everyone else being schooled there, I was cast even more as an outsider. I started feeling very angry about being the one who had to move and rebellion was a natural reaction to this displacement. I didn't understand why I should be the one getting up an hour and a half earlier to go to a school that far away. It was a 20-minute walk to and from the train station, then a 40-minute train journey each way, followed by a 30-minute walk to and from the station at the other end to the school. By the time I had arrived at the school gates, I was already exhausted and I arrived home in the evenings, shattered.

In contrast to my previous school, this one did not have a strict regime. During my first week there, someone took it upon themselves to smash in all the windows of the on-site greenhouse. I thought this was jolly good fun, and took this as a signal that I could behave in any manner I wanted. My rebellious self reached total fruition. Towards the end of the first week at my new school, another girl and I dared a first-year to steal a box of Roses chocolates out of a local shop. Mission accomplished, we all tucked into this feast on the way to school that morning. Not an easy task to polish them off between the three of us. This created its own little problem. The first-year girl was consequently sick in school and had to explain why. She *grassed* on us two older girls. So here I was, I hadn't been there a week and my card was already marked.

Rebels never seem to be alone so I had two really good friends there. Lindsay was prim and proper. Looking at the meanings of names, I found it funny that hers can either be taken as 'hotter than the flames of hell' or 'the marvellous and mysterious temptress from the land of eternal joy'. These words didn't sum her up at all. My other best mate was Lynn, who was into heavy metal and came from a home with lots of problems. I guess I just added to them. Lindsay would take my lead, and clown about in class. She would have me in fits of giggles but knew when to cut it out and face the front. As for me, I would continue to mess around and was always the one getting into trouble.

Lynn was my *mitching* partner. That was our term for it - you probably know it as *bunking off* or if you are more refined *playing truant*. On many occasions, we would go through the front door of the school and then straight out the back door. As a parent now, the concerning thing was that no-one seemed to notice. I guess you could say formal education wasn't my scene. I left school as soon as I could with several qualifications, but nothing to write home about.

A lack of qualifications didn't stop me having my own dreams, and I knew what I wanted to do. I fought for and secured a place in a drama school, but my mother advised me against it. 'There is no future in acting, no money to be made,' she said. We had a long talk and I eventually caved in. That remains one of the times I wish I hadn't listened to her. Instead, I found myself in a boring place, Rupert Stanley, doing a secretarial course. I wasn't happy at all. I found it all so uninteresting and my mind would wander off, fantasising on what I could be doing instead. More further education followed and I applied for a hotel receptionist course.

At the time, I met a soldier called Steven. I judged the man not the uniform he wore but I was more than aware that many people looked upon him as the *enemy*. People were talking behind my back and the relationship was frowned upon in certain quarters. I had met Steven in a nightclub. He said I was different and that I wasn't *like the other girls*. These days I would have blown a raspberry in his face for such a corny approach, but at the time it was exactly what I wanted to hear. He was five years older than me and had decided he was ready for settling down. My father didn't like him, which just demonstrates how perceptive he was. Of course, that made me like Steven even more, the little rebel in me coming out in spades. As wise parents know, it's never advisable to comment on the romantic choices of your sons and daughters. Just let it ride, see where the pieces land and be there to pick them up when needed.

Not long after I started going out officially with Steven, I had gone out to Toomebridge, a small village on the northwest corner of Lough Neagh in County Antrim, with my friend Geraldine to meet with her cousins. I noticed the hostility almost immediately. Geraldine's cousins were bitchy and catty to me, it was heading ever closer to downright aggression. Unbeknown to me, Geraldine had told them I was going out with a British soldier. A cardinal sin. I saw nothing wrong with this, but that was enough for them to warrant what happened next.

Geraldine and I were in a parked car near Lough Neagh with two male friends when we became aware that the car was surrounded by her cousins and at least three or four other girls that I didn't know. Before I knew what was happening someone had pulled my door open and I found myself being dragged out by my hair. They were on me like ants on a piece of dead meat. As they kicked and punched and screamed abuse, I was aware of one of the boys and Geraldine dragging the girls off me but as soon as they pulled one body away, another girl took her place. The sustained attack seemed to go on forever as I begged for mercy. Eventually, they decided I had had enough as I lay dazed, bloody and barely conscious. Geraldine cleaned me up and one of the boys drove me home to Geraldine's grandmother's house where I spent the night. I cried the whole way, totally in shock at the animalistic behaviour of these girls. In a way, the shock at what they had been capable of was more than the physical pain.

To add insult to injury, the next day they had the brass neck to come around to Geraldine's grandmother's, and apologise to me. Like a fool I forgave them. I think Geraldine had tipped them off that I was going to get the police involved. I still remember this as if it were yesterday. It's one part of my life that I can never forget no matter how hard I try.

I was traumatised after that beating. Although it was very out-of-character, I took myself off to England with my boyfriend. What was I thinking? I was in such an emotional state, and with dad not liking him much, I just didn't feel like *Daddy's girl* anymore. With my father and others, putting so many fleas in my ears, enough was enough. I stamped my foot and barked, 'Fuck this, I'm outta here,' and I left the family home. A big mistake.

We stayed in several of Steven's friends' homes until we eventually married and got our own army house. I was hoping for a sense of community when I moved in. Fat chance, as I felt lonely as well as vulnerable and all the other army wives were bitchy to me. I know some of them viewed me as the enemy because I was an Irish Catholic. I remember thinking - Jeez, you can't win. But there was something else too. Some of the girls had let themselves go, they were very plain and some of them looked as if they just didn't want to make any sort of an effort to look nice. I was the complete opposite and I think some of them didn't like the fact that a younger, more presentable girl had dared to step foot into their world.

That was their problem with self-confidence, not mine, but of course, who was going to get the raw end of this deal? My mane of black hair was something of a beacon. I admit that many boys had chatted me up by saying I should be a model. At the time, I'd always laughed at that idea, but maybe the army wives thought the same thing. Perhaps their husbands had been daft enough to make similar comments. I wasn't interested in anyone if truth be told, especially other *squaddies*.

Within a very short time, I wanted to go home. I was homesick, but I was trapped, having burned my bridges. I hadn't even told mum and dad I was now married. I got hitched behind their backs. Steven, being a soldier, was away on 24-hour duties and sometimes I didn't see him for weeks at a time. Often he was posted to different countries. All I wanted was a friend to talk to, but I made none. It was hostile isolation.

2

Euphoria and Heartache

Like many young women, I thought I had the answer. I became pregnant and was really happy. I thought Steven would be happy too but how wrong I was. Despite him having made such an issue of wanting to settle down, he now grouched at me moaning that he wasn't ready to have a family. Didn't I realise I would be left alone with the baby while he was travelling around the world? He wouldn't budge on this and under no circumstances did he want me to have his child. I was distraught and had no-one to turn to. The decision was made for me and I was to have a termination. His mind was made up. If I'd adhered more to my Catholic upbringing, that would have added further to my dilemma.

The experience of getting to the hospital holds no great memories. However, as the mist caused by being anaesthetised cleared, I woke up from my abortion with a jump. Distraught. Dizzy. Confused. Beside me was a large pregnant woman who was just about to give birth. I wasn't that far gone not to be shocked at how insensitive the medical staff were here. Did they not realise they had put me beside a woman who was giving birth and to her sixth child at that? I shook my head and gritted my teeth in a mixture of anger and bewilderment. I remember getting a taxi back home. I got the driver to stop off, so that I could get fish and chips and a large box of After Eight mints, my comfort food. I needed to fill the emotional and physical emptiness I now felt inside.

That incident was the trigger that started my run-in with bulimia.

I was bleeding heavily for a while after the termination. I couldn't speak to anyone and I became a recluse, staying in the house alone for several weeks at a time. I was lonely and frightened and even started getting panic attacks. I didn't have a phone in the house and, despite there being a phone box nearby, I remained a prisoner of my own making. It was no surprise that I slumped into a deep depression. Some might even have called it a breakdown. Things were to get even worse because I just couldn't cope anymore. Somewhere in the recesses of my mind, it made sense to cut my arms and finally I was in control of the pain.

Less than two years after signing up for life as an army wife, I was resolute enough to accept how homesick I was. Steven bought himself out of the army and relocated over to Northern Ireland. I swallowed my pride and moved back home. I managed to get a job with an alarm company which paid quite well. Steven became a delivery driver and, although he wasn't on huge wages, our combined incomes were enough to allow us to buy a house. Finally, after listening to all those compliments I'd been paid over the years, I also secured some freelance modelling jobs and began to get a bit of recognition. Part of me liked the attention although at times it was scary to be recognised by people I'd never met and didn't know. I was featured in the Sunday World and other newspapers, draping myself over various cars at motor shows; anything to bring in the sales for the manufacturers.

The work brought me mainstream attention and I even had Mayfair and Penthouse wanting to stage lucrative photo-shoots that would reveal all of me, but I wouldn't even go topless. I was too prudish at the time and worried about what my family and friends would have thought. I wasn't prepared to find out and although both magazines rang me several times the answer was always, 'No!' If I was asked now and had the figure I had then, well, who knows. Times have certainly changed.

Although Steven didn't say a lot when the magazines called me, I wasn't sure how he would feel about other blokes seeing more of me in pictures than they would in real life. I laughed to myself because the devil in me could only imagine how much it would have wound up the wives of those *squaddies* who had made my life so tough.

Steven and I were settled in our new house for only a few months when we decided our relationship was going nowhere. I knew it had been a big mistake but didn't want to admit defeat. However, I finally realised I had to accept I wasn't getting on with my husband anymore. We were arguing and fighting quite a lot by then. I knew it was over and resented him because of his reaction to my pregnancy. I was having flashbacks to the termination. I felt bitter about how he had pressurised me into having that abortion. I would shout and scream at him. I'm surprised the neighbours didn't report it. It was predictable that we would split up and Steven wasted no time in moving back to England. After the split, I was very lonely and I missed him but I knew there was no going back. Divorce was inevitable.

The following year I met Kevin and within six months I was pregnant. It was one of the happiest times of my life. On Saturday 27 March 1993 my *little bundle of joy* arrived. Miss Sophia Lorraine said hello to the world. Kevin was delighted to be her dad, how different to what I'd experienced up until then. This was undoubtedly the best day of my life. My darling baby was named after one of my favourite movie stars, Sophia Loren. Sophia made her debut at 6lbs 7oz, with a little mop of black hair. I was so glad the genes had fallen that way.

When Sophia was born, the midwife, an Indian lady, was mesmerised with my child. She kept stating over and over again what long limbs she had, what a beautiful baby she was and what defined features she had. She doted on her finely-toned leg muscles. She even marvelled at how lean and long her fingers were. I was on such a high for months to come. My elation was such that I decided to become a stay-at-home mum. My girl was going to get all my attention. I had waited five years for her to come along, since the date of that termination. I'd never stopped dreaming of bringing a new life to planet Earth and Sophia didn't disappoint.

Life was magical around that time. Sophia was the perfect baby who grew into a beautiful child. I pushed her around in her pram for hours and enjoyed playing with her on the beaches of the stunning Antrim coastline. She was always full of energy and the summers were warm and long. She learned to cycle and I would walk or run alongside her bike for miles. One day we set off from the house as usual, me on foot, Sophia on her bike. As we walked out of the estate I noticed a man standing by a small motorcycle, a scrambler bike with high mudguards. He was dressed in black leathers and I remember thinking how hot he must have been. He was also wearing his full-face crash helmet which I remember thinking was a little strange as the bike was stationary and the engine silent.

I thought nothing more of it and concentrated on Sophia telling her to stay on the pavement. I'd walked less than a mile to where the same motorbike was parked beside the Brown Cow pub. I walked by and, after no more than a minute, someone grabbed me from behind. I was taken by surprise and in complete shock. I remember screaming and watched Sophia fall from her bike as it careered into the road. My initial concern was for Sophia but, within seconds, I realised he had no interest in my child. He had his left arm locked around me leaving his right hand free. We struggled as I fought back and we stumbled onto a grass verge where I lost my footing. I fought back as he grabbed me between my legs. I don't think the ordeal lasted more than a minute or two and, because Sophia's bike was in the middle of the road blocking it, I became aware of a car horn. The driver probably didn´t realise what was going on but that was enough. The car horn blared again and the man jumped up and ran to his bike. He kicked the engine into life and was gone. A lady ran up to me and said she had witnessed everything then she took Sophia and me to the police station. I was in hysterics as was Sophia but I tried to calm her down, telling her it was nothing and that mummy was fine. As the lady drove me home I remember thinking that the bike and the man seemed familiar to me.

My happiness didn't last. Kevin and I had our troubles and we agreed to separate for a time although I was still fond of him. The separation lasted a while; so much so that he bought his own house and I bought mine. The arrangement worked well and we were still seeing each other on an almost daily basis which was fine. He was very much a hands-on father and I could never be accused of limiting the time he spent with his daughter.

3

An Innocent Request, my Journey into Hell

The adventures in Kevin's street began in May 2005. His large bungalow was in an estate in Langford Close. It had a nice initial vibe and Sophia and I were only too happy to visit it as often as we could. She had a bedroom there that looked out onto the small turning area at the end of the cul-de-sac. Kevin had been in the house for a few weeks when one of the neighbours decided to introduce herself. I thought it was strange because that's normally the sort of thing you would have done within the first day or two of a neighbour moving in. Kevin's car was in the driveway. I had walked down from my house to see him and I was in the kitchen, but the lady didn't know we were there. Sophia had a view of the whole street and she noticed this small matriarch woman around 5 feet tall with dark hair and brown eyes talking to Kevin by his car in the driveway. She had a bottle of red wine in one hand.

I smiled to myself. I thought - This is nothing unusual, just a neighbour introducing herself. She was smiling at Kevin. Although I caught snatches of the conversation, I wasn't that interested. I thought I would be sociable and decided to get acquainted too. As I walked out, she looked up but her face dropped. I've always been very intuitive and immediately got a very bad vibe from her. Nevertheless, she smiled as she turned towards me, 'Hi, I'm Denise Black. I'm just talking to your husband here, introducing myself.'
'Diane Taylor,' I responded as I shook her hand.
'My husband's away on a golfing weekend,' she added which set the alarm bells ringing. She and her husband had had ample opportunity to introduce themselves. Why would she decide to get acquainted when her husband was away?
Then, for no good reason, she mentioned that she had friends working for the British Broadcasting

Corporation (BBC) or it could have been Ulster Television (UTV). It was irrelevant and nothing at all to do with what we had been talking about. What was that all about? She *harrumphed*, spun on her heels and curtly said, 'Anyway, must dash. I'm in a hurry; we can have a chat some other time.' As she walked across the road, I looked at Kevin as he raised an eyebrow.

I thought to myself – Strange.

Nevertheless, it was a nice gesture and better late than never. I even sent her a Christmas card, to encourage the potential friendship, from Kevin, Sophia and myself. Little did I know the horror that was about to unfold.

In January 2006, Kevin realised his home was worth a lot more than he'd originally paid for it. It was that time in the decade where property prices were rocketing. So, he decided to release some equity, as they say in mortgage terms, providing funds to renovate the house and make some home improvements. He'd mentioned putting a porch on the front of the house. First of all, he was on a mission to change the paintwork and wallpaper to make the house feel like a home. To begin with, he painted the hall a pale shade of cream. A few days after he had finished, I noticed someone painting the hallway of Denise Black's house. Her front door was open and I couldn't help but notice, in great contrast to Kevin's hall, Denise Black's was a deep burgundy colour. It didn't remain that shade for long and, as the painter progressed, I could see that he was changing the colour to a similar tint of cream to Kevin's.

I wasn't concerned at all and thought nothing of it at the time. As the weather improved Kevin spent a few hundred pounds on plants and hanging baskets for the front of the house. It gave much-needed colour to the front street. A few days later the Blacks followed suit by putting similar plants outside their home. This was strange. I told Kevin to hang fire with any improvements for the time being.

Kevin's shellfish business was doing very well. His exports to Spain had jumped up to another level and he decided to treat himself to a new Jet Ski, something he had wanted since he was a small child. Within a few weeks, the Blacks had a sizeable cruiser boat sitting right outside their home. Denise Black spent a fair bit of time on that boat, doing small repairs and cleaning it. Whenever we entered or left the house, she would make a point of sarcastically waving at us. Her behaviour was beginning to concern us but we said nothing. 'Live and let live,' Kevin said. 'She isn't doing us any harm.'

We were also noticing some other unusual behaviour from over the road. It was as if her husband was scared to look across at our house. When he wasn't there, the blinds would be open. She would stand in the hall where we could see her, with her phone in her hand talking and looking over. I told myself again and again - Let it go.

She was, undoubtedly, a woman of temperament and bad mood swings. It was obvious when she was in a mood because she would drive erratically. She'd squeal off the driveway in her car and zoom away with the engine revving at high speed. Little did I know, but I was about to push Denise Black to the next level and see her temperament first hand. Our neighbourhood dispute was about to begin.

It was an innocuous request. Sophia had been complaining about the car headlights and the noise from cars in the cul-de-sac turning point which was adjacent to her bedroom. The street had plenty of parking spaces and every drive had enough space for one or two cars. Indeed the Black's driveway was bigger than most with enough space for half a dozen cars. However, the Blacks and their friends seemed to be parking more often in the turning circle. It wasn't a major problem during the day (other than causing inconvenience to people turning around) but in the evening, when Sophia was trying to sleep it was a bloody nuisance.

I caught Denise one Monday morning, after a particularly hectic weekend when several of her friends had been back and forward to the house, some leaving in the early hours of the morning.

I was pleasant enough as I spoke to her and mentioned, 'I hope you don't mind but I would be grateful if your friends could park elsewhere.'

'And why is that?' she asked.

I explained about Sophia, how she was having trouble sleeping. I politely pointed out that it was a turning circle, not a car park.

'So if you don't mind,' I said.

'Well I do mind,' she retorted, 'you don't own the bloody road.'

I was speechless. I was not expecting that response. If the shoe had been on the other foot I would have apologised profusely and assured my neighbour that it would not happen again. Before I could even take in what she had said she was gone, marching away like a drill sergeant on parade. The negotiations had broken down and, as far as Denise Black was concerned, it was a declaration of war. Never did I realise the full extent that harmless request would have on my life and that of my family.

It appeared that not only had Denise Black started a war, but also she had encouraged her friends and family to declare war too. I dread to think what she told them because her friends' behaviour changed. Whereas before I had hardly noticed them, they now made a point of deliberately driving as slowly as they could past our house. They'd stare in, beep their car horns, wave at me and then drive off. I'd had worse than that happen to me in the past and made a vow to myself that their intimidation was not going to work on me.

A few days later, Denise Black also turned on Kevin while he was in his driveway minding his own business, working on his Jet Ski. She walked past with her husband, stopped at the bottom of the drive and started ranting and screaming at Kevin. He was dumbfounded and stood there speechless. It seemed she was making up laws in her head, something about how it was illegal to work on machinery in a private estate. Her husband had to calm her down and drag her away. Kevin said the husband seemed to be embarrassed by her erratic behaviour.

One incident was very memorable. My father was with Kevin in the hallway with the door open while I was in the bedroom getting something from a drawer. My father and Kevin noticed Denise Black driving slowly past, almost breaking her neck staring into our house. It was her usual *nosey parker* routine that we had decided to ignore. She stalled her car right outside Kevin's house and it wouldn't start up again. Eventually, she climbed out and started ranting at Kevin and dad, is if it were somehow their fault. Again they ignored her, closed the door and walked away. They were even laughing about it in the kitchen but I confess her downward spiral of behaviour was beginning to worry me.

I liked to keep fit and did a lot of walking. I'd wear some high-cut shorts, making the best of my long tanned legs, taking in the beautiful clean air along the nearby shore. Denise was able to see me from the front of her house as she had a sea view property and we would bump into each other a lot. Sometimes she would beep her horn, sometimes she would wave sarcastically and other times she would stare straight ahead and do nothing, sour-faced at the wheel as I walked along the road. Often as I returned from my walk or a run, she would be standing in the window with her children, pointing and ranting angrily at me, though I couldn't hear a word she was saying. Her facial gestures and hand signals made up for my inability to lip-read. I thought - What a fruitcake. I picked up my pace and jogged on. It was only a matter of time before things escalated. I could almost feel Denise Black's frustration as I refused to rise to her bait and ignored everything she threw at me.

A couple of days later as I was getting into my Jeep to go and see Kevin down at the beach, I noticed the Blacks walking over the road towards me. Sophia was in the house watching TV, I had told her I would be away no longer than half an hour. I climbed into the car and tried to gauge their mood. Were they coming over on a peace mission, to bury the hatchet? They weren't. Just as I was about to wind the window down Denise began to rant and shouted out a tirade of abuse. What had I done? We hadn't reported them, hadn't made any complaints to the police. What could she possibly be upset about? And boy was she upset. She stood pressed up against the driver's door snarling at me and I edged away from her. As I did so, her husband stood in front of the car. They were both shouting and I couldn't drive forward or get out of the driver's side. Flashbacks of being trapped in the car in Toomebridge savaged my senses.

To escape the Blacks, I crawled out of the passenger door and on to Kevin's grass verge. They both charged after me and tried to corner me. Their goal was obviously to frighten me but at the time I sincerely believed Mr Black was going to attack me. He was in my face screaming, 'What did you say to my wife?' He repeated that over and over again. I was palpitating with fear; I hadn't said anything to her.

I howled, 'You haven't a clue what she's like! She's an evil bitch!'

That stunned him, and his hesitation allowed me the chance to run back into the bungalow. Sophia was on-hand to witness my distressed state. I waited until the Blacks went back into their house and told Sophia I was going to see her dad. I was so upset and distressed while tears rolled down my face.

When I got to the beach, Kevin was thankfully able to calm me down and persuaded me that it would eventually pass, they would get tired or bored, that it couldn't last forever. Although I didn't know at the time, this was the day that Denise Black contacted the police and told them my child was in danger. There was no earthly reason why she should do this, but she did. The local police seemed to take what she said as gospel from the very beginning and they telephoned Social Services to report a complaint. I was lucky at that point, as Social Services dismissed this referral closing the case the same day. I must note at this point I did not find out about this referral until 2011, nearly five years later, and that there had also been other things going on behind the scenes, incidents that were reported that I knew nothing about until much later. It was all rather sinister like something from a psychological thriller on Netflix.

I tried to put this last incident behind me and, for a while, it all went quiet. Several weeks after the very first *verbal*, her brother, Dr Haslam, parked in the same contentious parking area which was the source of our first disagreement. I had had enough. As I looked over at the Blacks' drive, I saw there was enough space for a double-decker bus but Dr Haslam decided to park outside my daughter's bedroom window. I confronted him. I may have been a little angry but I asked him nicely to park on his sister's drive as my daughter was in bed trying to get to sleep. He looked at me as if I was something he had scraped off his shoe and then mumbled something about me being *psychologically disturbed*. Before I could answer he climbed in his car and drove off.

Unbeknown to me, Dr Haslam reported the incident to the police. He accused me of harassment and, four days after this disagreement about where he should park, someone also made another telephone call to what I assume was a Mental Health Trust hospital and made a recommendation that I should be sectioned under the Mental Health Act (MHA). For those of you who don't know, an individual can only be sectioned under the MHA if they pose a danger to themselves or others. Dr Haslam had called me *psychologically disturbed*, those words had been particularly hurtful, and I wondered if it had been Dr Haslam who had referred me to the Mental Health Authority. On what possible grounds would anybody want me sectioned?

I had spoken to Dr Haslam for no more than 30 seconds and during the conversation, I didn't even raise my voice. No one in the immediate vicinity was in any danger. It was, at best, a disgracefully unprofessional act from someone trying to use their position of respect and authority for personal reasons.

Once again, although I didn't know at the time, this attempt to have me sectioned was referred to my own doctor who sent them packing and dismissed the ludicrous allegation. These people were deliberately making accusations up in their heads, getting involved in my private life and the police were taking them at face value.

Coincidently, I went to see my own doctor, Dr Dixon around this time. He told me about the referral but said not to worry. He said the practice had dismissed it as pathetic and told them in no uncertain terms that it was a figment of someone's imagination. There was nothing wrong with me, and it was against my human rights. He put it on record that I was having a stressful time with my neighbours. Thankfully I had a great relationship with Dr Dixon because, as a teenager, a traumatic event had led me to self-harm. He comforted me and said, 'Diane, you had a little temper tantrum as a teenager. Stop worrying yourself about this.'

Dr Dixon always had a way of making me feel better and suggested that I contact a solicitor who would send a letter to the Blacks informing them of the parking restrictions within the turning circle in the cul-de-sac. 'That should sort everything out,' he said. I took him up on his advice and contacted a solicitor who sent the Blacks a letter. At the same time, Kevin suggested we voluntarily go to the local police station to explain what had been happening, to put it on record, in case the neighbourhood dispute escalated.

Yet one thing was still bugging me, the fact that Dr Haslam had called me *psychologically disturbed* and had made a real attempt to have me sectioned under the MHA. I later found out he had declared to the Mental Health Team that I was psychotic, delusional, and prone to bizarre behaviour. He even feared I would self-harm. Those nasty, angry, unsubstantiated words left me worried about the course of events up to that point.

4

Skullduggery

Several weeks had passed since Dr Haslam had attempted to have me sectioned. Little did I know that more false statements were being manufactured. Just when I thought everything had settled down, Dr Haslam came back to our street with a police officer. His name was Peter Black who was a family member of the Blacks. You couldn't make this up! They deliberately parked in the same controversial parking area and began walking around and around their vehicle. Next, they started opening and closing the doors on both sides. It went on and on. Just what were they up to?

They stood on Kevin's grass verge right beside the turning area next to Sophia's bedroom window. There they anchored themselves, laughing loudly and staring in at Sophia who was in her room. Pesky, menacing behaviour especially as it was directed at an under-age girl. It just seemed so petty but was deliberate and provocative. They saw we had spotted them and left with churlish smiles on their faces.

A few hours later, a pair of police officers called at the bungalow. We were informed that another complaint had been made against us, this time from Dr Haslam and Peter Black. We had allegedly harassed them. Kevin and I decided this was enough to force our hand. Consequently, on 17 September 2006, we arrived at the police station. This time to lodge our counter-complaint, to put on record how ridiculously childish Dr Haslam and Peter Black were being. We were put into the care of Police Constable (PC) Noel Teeney, a stick-thin man with reddish-blonde hair. Taking on the role of good cop, PC Teeney took us into the incident room. We sat down and Kevin resolutely informed him of what had happened and that we were there to make our statement of complaint. PC Teeney took in a sharp intake of breath and began shaking his head. Kevin continued. We had evidence to submit, detailing what they had done but this didn't seem to tip the balance. As he leaned over, PC Teeney quietly enquired if we had any idea how senior Peter Black was in the force. Not picking up the intimation we wondered why that would have been so important. He stated again that we didn't want to go there by making a complaint against him.

PC Teeney suggested we would do better talking through the issues with him. We could state what the problem with the parking consisted of and he'd then make up a list of suggested resolutions. These could be submitted to the Blacks for their agreement. He called this a 'wish list' for both parties. It seemed reasonable so we detailed what had been going on and PC Teeney scribbled down the points we made (or so we thought). It felt like a fairly positive experience. We got down to brass tacks stuff, like the Blacks not parking their cars on our side of the road, and us not parking on their side of the road. It all seemed so obvious and at last, I felt we were making headway. PC Teeney then asked us to sign the completed piece of paper, a reasonable request. We both naïvely did so and sincerely believed this was an agreement to play our part in helping to bring this neighbourhood dispute to an end.

Things settled down for a while, both Kevin and I dared to think that the solicitor's letter and the interview with PC Teeney, may have done the trick. We were sadly mistaken. Another PC turned up at the house and stated that the police had received a complaint that I had been waving sarcastically at Diane Black and her kids. I couldn't quite believe it. 'Waving sarcastically?' I questioned. 'Is that a criminal offence?' He told me to stop being clever saying that I had upset Mrs Black's children.

He quoted one child as saying, 'Mummy, mummy, the lady is going to get you.'

I was at the end of my tether. I thought - Somebody tell me this isn't happening.

I'd had enough. I tried to explain this was a minor neighbourhood dispute over parking and that it was escalating to ridiculous levels. I questioned why the PC was even there and didn't he have better things to do. I was determined to put a stop to this once and for all, so Sophia and I drove to the police station and sat in the reception area. PC Wooton appeared, nice and amiable, and invited me to go into the interview room. I was asked if I knew why I was there then the bombshell was dropped. I was about to receive another caution for waving sarcastically as I had upset the Black's kids. 'Another caution?' I asked, confused. 'I haven't ever been cautioned.'

'Yes, you have,' he said. 'The one Officer Teeney gave you.'

The penny dropped. I was furious. PC Teeney had asked me to sign a piece of paper when we explained to him about what had been happening with our neighbours. The word caution was never mentioned. Looking back at these sequences of events in the cold light of day, I believe this was the very moment when fear crept in and the very real realisation that I was mixed up in something that was beyond my control. A police officer had tricked me into signing something that had no relevance to the interview that had taken place. Police officers didn't do that sort of thing, or did they? PC Wooton spoke again. 'You just need to sign the caution and then you can be on your way.' I asked if the procedure could be put on hold to wait for Kevin to arrive. This was agreed, so I went back to Sophia and we huddled together in the foyer.

We then heard a Sergeant (Sgt) McConnell shouting at PC Wooton, demanding he hurry up and get me cautioned. He came charging out like a bull in a china shop demanding we get on with it. I said, 'No, you said we could wait for Sophia's daddy to arrive.' PC Wooton grabbed me by the arm and starting shaking me. 'I am cautioning you for harassing Denise Black,' he blustered.

I was horrified and responded, 'Take your hands off me. I'm not a common criminal.'

He tightened his grip.

'You're assaulting me in front of my daughter,' I screamed. At that point, thankfully, Kevin appeared. He was furious.

'Did I just see you assaulting her, and threatening to arrest her?' he asked.

Kevin demanded PC Wooton's number from the Sergeant behind the desk. Kevin made a quick statement and we were then allowed to leave. We went back home in two cars. I was livid and sent an email out to Carrickfergus Police. I'd had enough, I was determined to go to the Police Ombudsman because of the assault, the harassment by our neighbours, and being generally bullied and victimised by those in a position of power.

5

Tit for Tat

The following day I went to the office of the Police Ombudsman. They took a statement and began their investigations. The neighbourhood dispute was so out of hand that both of us were making tit for tat complaints. I never wanted to make my complaints but felt compelled to do so otherwise it would have looked like a one-sided affair. I knew Denise Black was making complaints almost weekly but it was, however, only Kevin and I who were being bullied and victimised by the police. You didn't need a mathematics degree to add up that this must have been because of Denise Black's connections. Since we had contact with the Police Ombudsman and, after the caution I had received whilst being assaulted by PC Wotton, we demanded that the Blacks be cautioned for harassing us.

On 5 December 2006 PC McVeigh cautioned Denise Black under the Harassment Act. We dared to dream that it might be the end of the hostilities but, on 12 December, the police turned up at my door and told me I had to report to the police station. They allowed me to call Kevin who told me not to panic and that he would be with me in 10 minutes. Kevin came home to take me to the police station immediately but this time I took my handheld camera along. I had purchased it the week before, determined to record evidence of harassment from the Blacks and Peter Black in particular. My sister advised me to do this, saying I had every right to record things. This didn't go down too well with the police. They weren't used to dealing with someone who knew their rights.

We arrived at the station and were greeted by Sgt Miskellia. He said, 'I'm afraid you are going to be arrested, Diane.' I thought it was a joke. I knew I'd done nothing wrong. I asked if he was going to handcuff me. He scoffed, saying that I was a lady and there was no need for that. I was taken in an unmarked police car to Antrim Police Station to be questioned. When we arrived, I was searched. That was followed by the usual arrest procedure with my belongings being taken off me. I was asked by PC McVeigh if I required a solicitor. I told him, 'No.' Surely there was no need because this could be cleared up quickly.

I discovered the basis of the complaint. Denise Black had accused me of intimidation because I had been standing talking to someone for 45 minutes inside the porch (basically a closed in conservatory) at Kevin's house. I remembered I had been talking to Simon, a real chatterbox, and I hadn't asked him into the house knowing that once he got comfortable he could have been there for hours. Of course, the porch looked onto the Black's house so she had accused me of malicious behaviour and staring over at her house in an intimidating manner. If it hadn't been so serious it would have been laughable.

I said I wished they'd had a lie detector test for this nonsense and it could be cleared up immediately. Little did I know such a test would help me restore my faith in my sanity.
I was on Slimfast at that time. I had put on some weight having been laid-up after damaging my right

ankle, so I was a little fuzzy and light-headed. I couldn't believe how ludicrous the situation had become. It was absurd, so much so that I was making a joke of it and being sarcastic. That didn't help my cause. Eventually, after signing the statement, they let me go and said it was unlikely to ever go to court. I thought to myself - What is the point?

We drove back home and went into the house via the porch, the same porch Denise Black had named to accuse me of intimidation. I shook my head in disbelief. I knew that I would never stand inside that porch again for more than a minute or two. No matter how hard I tried to ignore it, Denise Black had a victory of sorts.

Kevin and I started to argue, and we felt we couldn't even look out of his front windows. I was living on my nerves. If Kevin was on the porch talking to someone, I would get very annoyed because I couldn't do the same, I'd become nervous and ask him to hurry up. The same thought invaded my head time and time again, that I had been arrested for standing inside a porch.

Denise Black may have stopped me from standing in Kevin's porch but I was determined that she wouldn't stop me from visiting his house. I still liked taking walks and, as Kevin lived just around the corner from me, walking to his house was a time I felt at peace. I always found it relaxing, where I could take in the scenery, feel the wind in my hair and generally forget about the nonsense that was going on with the Blacks.

On one of these walks to Kevin's house, I was aware of a white transit van that had driven past me, it seemed to slow down and, as I looked up, I noticed it had parked at the Carrickfergus KFC car park, 100 yards away alongside the footpath. Something made me feel uncomfortable and I slowed down as I approached the van. I could see a man in the driver's seat. The footpath was slightly raised from the road so, as I drew level with the van, I could see into the cab. The man stared out at me with a wicked grin on his face. His trousers were down at his knees and he was masturbating. As he saw the look of shock on my face this seemed to spur him on and he thrust his hips out, lifting his backside from the seat to ensure I had the perfect view of his erect penis and the act he was committing. I was frozen in shock for a second. He was getting a kick and didn't let up. I reached for my phone and called Kevin in a panic. Within a few minutes, Kevin arrived and startled the man who drove off. Kevin chased after him but he disappeared into a dead end. Kevin thought better of approaching him and instead took his registration number.

Kevin insisted that we report the incident to the police despite me not trusting them anymore. The pervert was eventually caught, arrested and admitted his guilt. He also had the brass neck to bring his girlfriend to the police station at the time he was being questioned. He told the police how sorry he was. His defence was that he was carrying out a sex act in the privacy of his own van, which was plain nonsense. He clearly got off on the fact it was witnessed by an unsuspecting female in broad daylight.

The Public Prosecution Service (PPS) decided a caution was sufficient retribution for him and it was not necessary to take him to court. Just another incident I found hard to come to terms with. He had gotten off with a caution, while I was being bullied and victimised by the police for nothing more than a minor tit for tat neighbourhood dispute. (This man didn't just stop masturbating in a van at the KFC or surrounding areas. Over the years he went on to repeat his performance in front of several more unsuspecting and shocked females. He once masturbated on a bus where the CCTV caught him. He was eventually sentenced to 14 months in prison, of which he only served half.)

In early March 2007, the Blacks were celebrating some event or other. A minibus drove into the cul-de-sac. Many of their friends got out of the vehicle, making a right racket. The minibus was parked in the corner of the turning circle and began flashing its lights several times into Sophia's bedroom window. I chose to ignore the incident and they eventually went inside to the party then drove off in the early hours of the morning.

My next shock was just a couple of weeks after that. I received a reply from the PPS. I recall the date well as it arrived on Sophia's birthday, 27 March 2007. In dismay, reading through all the statements they'd enclosed, they told me that the case was proceeding to court. I couldn't believe it and hastily drove out to see my sister Tanya, who was in the police service. She did not want to get involved. She scolded me, 'I warned you, didn't I? You don't mess with these people.'

For the first time in a long while, I was petrified. Just who were these people and how could they wield this level of power?

6

My First Day in Court

I first appeared in court on 19 December 2007 and
was convicted on the biggest pack of lies ever told. It
was almost embarrassing to hear the so called
harassment charges read aloud. They used words
like petty nonsense, verbal provocation, intimidating
waving and standing in a porch animated. It was all
rather bemusing and, as far as I was concerned, lies
and false statements from the Blacks' friends and
family. All of their family members, including Dr
Haslam (Black's brother-in-law), the police officer

and their friends, testified against me. One by one they wheeled them out. They took the stand and lied. Whenever Dr Haslam took the stand my barrister asked him, 'Doctor, did you contact anyone in regards to Diane Taylor's mental state of health?'

Dr Haslam blurted out, 'No sir.'

This question was repeated again and Dr Haslam once more replied, 'No sir.'

I stood up in court and stated that Dr Haslam had perjured himself. There was a deathly silence in the court room. The prosecuting barrister then handed a sheet of A4 paper to the judge which stated that it was, in actual fact, Carrickfergus Police who had referred me to a Community Mental Health Trust (CMHT). This in itself was wrong. The police need a doctor to make a referral, and no police doctor had ever seen me.

Denise Black had also tried to get other neighbours to testify against me in court. They proved to be impartial and would not get involved in such a petty dispute. This echoed my thoughts exactly - Why are we wasting time and money on such minor disagreements? This was not why the justice system was founded in the first place. I knew I was in trouble given the parade of witnesses who testified against me and, despite all the suspect evidence, the judge gave me a suspended sentence and told me that he wanted me back in a few weeks. He left me in no doubt that I would be receiving a custodial sentence. Prison. I thought to myself – Prison, you have to be joking! I looked over at Denise Black, she was grinning like a Cheshire cat. She requested that the judge remove me from Kevin's home so that I wouldn't cause any trouble. She said the bungalow was in my boyfriend's name and I didn't belong there anyway. At this point, the judge looked totally bemused and told her the point of a suspended sentence was for exactly that reason.

I went back to Kevin's house following the hearing. I was in a state of shock. I felt something had died inside of me that day. As a result, I felt very ill. A whole range of emotions was going through my head. Even worse was what was happening outside. I couldn't quite believe that Denise Black and her husband were staging a serious soap opera. They stood on the driveway of their house with the biggest bottle of champagne I think I've ever seen. They held up their glasses in my direction to toast their victory over my conviction. I couldn't believe it was the action of sane people. They were cheering and slapping each other on the back. I cried my eyes out and had a decision to make. I told Kevin I could no longer stay at his house, as I knew Denise Black would escalate her sick, twisted games, and make it unbearable for me to live there now that I was seen as the guilty party.

Kevin put his foot down and said I was staying put, regardless. He insisted, 'That evil bitch will not be driving you away from my house.' A week later, he took me on holiday to New York to help try and clear my head. Although some of the holiday was enjoyable, most of the time all I could think of was Judge Ken Nixon's voice, ringing like an alarm bell in my head, 'You will receive a custodial sentence.' With that phrase churning round and round, it simply ruined the break. I was upset that I'd been set up, that they'd got one over on me. All of it was totally out of my control. I was dizzy and disorientated due to the stress the injustice created.

When we returned, I told my solicitors their services would no longer be required. They had let me down by telling me, 'This nonsense will be thrown out of court.' I was annoyed that they hadn't called even one of my witnesses to court to give evidence. I decided to lodge an appeal with the court but I was not confident of the result. When no lawyer or barrister would take my case, and believe you me I tried to get one, there was only one thing to do. Contact a newspaper.

I phoned several titles, but only the Sunday World would pick up my story. I also contacted my Member of Parliament (MP), Sammy Wilson, concerning the evidence Dr Haslam had given in court. Sammy wrote to the PPS and the General Medical Council (GMC) with misconduct allegations. The PPS wrote back to Sammy and stated that, 'As there was an appeal listed for a hearing, any questions regarding perjury or misconduct allegations should be addressed in court'.

I realised I had to find another solicitor and thought my luck was in when I met up with Kevin Winters. He seemed sympathetic to my cause. We got off to a flying start when he told me I did not need to see a Probation Officer (PO) because I was lodging an appeal.

When I got to court to be sentenced I was appalled when Kevin Winters just dropped me at the court door. Rather than accompanying me, he had lined up a man named Finucane. He was the son of Pat Finucane a solicitor who had been murdered by paramilitary loyalists years previously. He told me they were going to drop me as a client too. I knew something was not right there. The firm of solicitors I had sacked were Madden & Finucane, and here was the son of one of those who not only worked for

Kevin Winters but also was informing me that they were not going to continue with the case.

I found myself in front of the judge with no legal representation and no PO report as requested. No wonder he was shouting at me. It was clear that I had better come into his court room next time with both a legal representative and a PO report! Off I went once more to find another firm of solicitors. Alas, they would be as disappointing as the others that had gone before them. I went to the PO as instructed but she was concerned with the statements I showed to her with regard to Denise Black's allegations. She wondered why there didn't appear to be any witnesses in these statements other than Denise Black's children.

The PO wrote her report and on 27 February 2008 I was in front of the judge for sentencing. I thought I was going to faint. I was shaking and crying, convinced I was going to prison.

I was given a six-month sentence, suspended for two years. I wasn't going to jail which was a relief, but it would still mean I would have this sentence hanging over me until 27 February 2010. Towards the end of proceedings, I couldn't help myself. I stood up and said to the judge, 'With all due respect, your Honour, you shouldn't be sentencing me. It's the Blacks and their family you should be sentencing for all their lies and perjury.'

The judge looked down at me, he seemed to sympathise. 'I understand,' he said, 'you are visibly shaken and upset and that's precisely why we have had that outburst, but please be seated.'

I sat down in dismay. I should have been feeling good because I wasn't going to prison but it was a hollow victory, I felt empty. I felt as if the world had conspired against me.

7

The Appeal

My appeal was in June 2008 and, casting my net widely, I was lucky to find a group of solicitors who I thought would be able to represent me. However, the day before court, I met with these solicitors and matters took a bizarre twist. Sophia was with me, and I could not believe what they said to her. They told me that they were not going to be dealing with the perjury allegations I had made or the referral that Dr Haslam made. They told me that I needed to sign a piece of paper, admit my guilt and get on with my life. I objected in the strongest possible terms. 'But this is an appeal against my conviction,' I said. Just what the hell was going on? They ignored my protests. One of them then addressed my daughter.

He said, 'Would you really like to visit your mummy in prison? Do you think your mummy would suit being in prison? We know how head-strong your mummy is, but you need to take your mummy aside and tell her to stop being so silly, sign a piece of paper, admit her guilt and get a small fine.'

Sophia was 15 at the time and was very upset as the tears began to fall. I took her home and told her not to worry. I would represent myself and no harm would come to me, I would not be going to prison.

The Sunday World sat in court with me as I took on the task of being my own legal representative in what was a three day appeal. Three days because of a neighbourhood disagreement over parking, and yet I was prepared to be there for three months if it meant clearing my name. It was all about the principle. The first day in court saw Denise Black ask Judge Corinne Philpott, to give her access to a video link-up. What happened next made me believe the judge was on my side. She was bemused by this request, and retorted: 'What do you think this is; a child sex abuse case?'

This was obviously Denise Black trying to *stack the deck* in her favour. I had never made any threats against her. Why the hell did she want to give evidence via a video link? It was as if we were in court to hear evidence from an IRA hit man. Meanwhile, Kevin spotted a man from the PPS who was at the back of the court. The judge would occasionally look his way, raising an eyebrow as if asking what the hell was this case doing in her court room.

The hearing commenced, and I asked the judge to throw the case out of court as my initial statement to the police had gone missing down the back of a shelf in Carrickfergus Police Station. I also pointed out to the judge that the Police Ombudsman had made recommendations relating to my case and regarded it as a petty neighbourhood dispute; it should not have been dragged into court. In fact, I told them I was the one who was being harassed, because of what Black's brother, Dr Haslam, had done, in both referring me to the CMHT and the inappropriate and unsubstantiated medical diagnosis he had submitted.

I informed the judge that Kevin and I had never been cautioned, as was stated, but tricked into signing a wish list. I asked to cross-examine PC Teeney. However, the judge said PC Teeney wasn't in court and therefore not available for cross-examination. The judge then kindly pointed out that it was in my legal right to subpoena PC Tenney but that I would have to put the court date off. I was eager to challenge all their lies but didn't want any more delays. Police officer Peter Black had turned up for court and I suggested on cross-examination that he had submitted a false statement. The judge became aware that his statement was indeed falsified. There were another nine witnesses who I was able to demonstrate were also lying. I did such a great job of representing myself that Judge Philpott complimented me to the other barrister Mr McCristie and stated what an exceptional job I was doing given the circumstances. I had gone into court that morning expecting my legal team to represent me but I ended up having to represent myself. I was only given around 30 minutes to prepare my case but that was enough time for me to underline all the lies in their false statements. The judge didn't throw the case out of court; however, she dismissed some of the charges against me.

During Kevin's cross-examination I objected to the prosecuting barrister, Mr McCristie, repeating a question to Kevin several times. I stood up and said, 'Objection Mr McCristie, you are badgering the witness.'

The judge looked down on me, rolled her eyes, and firmly told me to sit down.

Exasperated, she said, 'This is NOT an American court room drama.' These days, I can see the funny side of this ticking off by the judge.

When Kevin had taken the stand he told the judge that I had only ever had a 10 second verbal altercation with Black, and the rest of it was made up drama and lies. He said that Denise Black would continue to make more false allegations. Judge Philpott spoke in response and said that if either party came back to her court room, there would be serious consequences for both parties.

In summing up, Judge Philpott believed that the parking behaviour was deliberately being used to upset us. She stated this was a premeditated act by Denise Black, her friends and relatives. Judge Philpott dropped the sentence of six months suspended for two years, down to four months suspended for two years. I was so frustrated after all my hard work that the case wasn't thrown out, but at least it had moved in the right direction.

I was no sooner out of the court door when a male and female solicitor approached me saying what an excellent job I had done in representing myself especially as Judge Philpott was a tough but fair judge, and that I should class it as a win.

The judge then gagged the Sunday World from being able to run the story. The paper had that overturned a few weeks later and ran the story of my court room drama on 31 July 2008.

8

Arrested Again

On 3 August 2008, the Sunday World followed up the story of me representing myself in court, with another one exposing Dr Haslam and his behaviour. No sooner was the ink dry in the newspaper than Denise Black had made a further false allegation and got me arrested.

It was Friday, 29 August 2008, the end of a Bank Holiday week. Sophia and I had enjoyed a holiday in Cyprus. It wasn't trepidation I was feeling that morning, it was more the predictable malaise you have after returning from a foreign holiday. Even at her young age of 15, the relationship between Sophia and I was more that of sisters than mother-daughter. Cyprus has a calming influence on all its visitors, life doesn't have any urgency and everything seems laid back. How different to my home in Northern Ireland. I was a little light-headed because I had had less than four hours sleep after getting off the plane but I needed to make an early start as Sophia was back at school that morning. We set off in the Jeep. I dropped her at the bus stop, and continued on to Kevin's bungalow. It must have been around 8.30 am when I pulled into the driveway. Getting out of the car, I looked skywards. Although it was dry, the dullness didn't lift my spirits. I smiled at the contrast to the Mediterranean.

Kevin greeted me at his door. He had contacted me whilst I was on holiday to say he had received a visit from the police. On the phone he had been in a panic, convinced they were calling to do something nasty to me. He was a lot calmer now. When the Sunday World ran the story about how I had represented myself at my appeal, I was quite proud of the way they'd covered the court dramas. It made me feel quite the hero.

We talked about the holiday over a morning cuppa. Kevin filled me in on the latest news about his business. So many options were presenting themselves to him; I was pleased with the way things were turning out, a little normality in the mad world that we were living in. Over our *builders blend* there was a sense of inner calm for both of us. Little did we realise this was the lull before the storm. Kevin popped outside. Then the doorbell rang. Opening the door, I focused on the people in front of me. To the left was the fair-haired PC Cullen with another person to his right.

Back in 2004, PC Cullen had come out to my house after it had been broken into. He was quite a handsome guy - fit, muscular, a tribal tattoo on his left arm. Back in the present, it actually took a few seconds for me to process that he had a head camera on his helmet. I later found out that they'd only just started to use these as part of a trial. It was a little disconcerting, to say the least. A third eye staring straight at me. Clearing his throat, PC Cullen announced, 'I'm here to talk about an allegation you made on ...'

He read the date out, but I had temporarily switched off. A million thoughts were racing through my head, all of these colliding together, creating what felt like mini-explosions in my brain. I'd been to court, it was all over. I'd even been to appeal. Just what the hell was he talking about?

After a momentary pause, I checked out the policewoman beside him who was around 5 feet tall with dark hair. I pulled myself together enough to invite both of them in. We all sat down in the kitchen and I asked if they wanted some tea. The policewoman said they were not allowed to accept refreshments.

I told them there had to have been some sort of mistake as I hadn't had any contact or dealings with the Blacks. PC Cullen revealed that an allegation had been made. I had harassed Denise Black. 'What, again?' I asked. 'What am I alleged to have done now and when? I've just returned from holiday. I haven't even been here.' My problem now was to try and work out what on earth this was about.

PC Cullen cleared his throat again and continued, 'I am afraid I am going to have to arrest you under the Harassment Act and you will have to come down to the station.'

I looked at the policewoman for some sort of reaction, maybe a clarification. I got nothing. Stone cold, she was looking through me. I wanted to curl up into a ball and die. Surely this wasn't happening again?

Stuttering and confused and on the verge of tears, I asked for a couple of minutes to go and change the top I'd been travelling in. They relented, and I made time to make a phone call to the Sunday World. Stephen Moore, their journalist, was now on my speed-dial. I spluttered to him that I was being arrested again and they wouldn't tell me why. Meanwhile Kevin was upset. Like me, he found the lack of an explanation an incredibly unreal experience. He followed the police officers and me out of the house, shaking his head. No doubt the neighbours, behind their net curtains, got the sort of eyeful they were always seeking, especially when I was bundled into the police 4x4. The policewoman drove the vehicle, and PC Cullen was on my right side in the rear. The camera-helmet was even more intrusive in this proximity. He was in my face with it, staring at me all the while.

Trying to second-guess what was coming next, I thought they would be taking me to Carrickfergus Police Station. I felt even more intimidated as we were driving really slowly. PC Cullen took a phone call; they told him to take me to Antrim Special Criminal Suite (ASCS). Gruffly-barked instructions were fired at the policewoman by PC Cullen. The route taken was down country lanes. By the time we drove up past the New Line, I was hyperventilating. It felt like their negative thoughts were crushing my head. They made me dizzy and distraught. I had done nothing wrong but stand up for myself and use my fight and determination. Then another inner voice reminded me I was standing up for what I believed in. Don't let them win. Justice must be done.

We had arrived at ASCS. I had seen the sign. The sun shone harshly into my eyes as I jumped out. From that point on, my recollections are a blur. When we got in to the building, I met, for the first time, Sgt Trevor Todd. As PC Cullen read out the allegations, you could see Sgt Todd's one eyebrow, then the other, being raised in a mixture of bemusement and amazement. The allegations were tittle-tattle, about me waving at Denise Black, and I quote, 'Gawping with *hard stares*' and 'standing in the porch with arms menacingly crossed.' These were old allegations being read out – I didn't hear anything new.

Sgt Todd looked to the heavens for inspiration, before tearing a strip off the PC. He wanted to know why I'd been bought to his station on such a minor matter. The implication was that this was a gross over-reaction to a trivial complaint. At this point, I demanded to speak to a doctor, annoyed at the distress I was being caused for what was now being considered, by Sgt Todd at least, no good reason.

Half an hour later a doctor arrived. He looked at me coldly as I told him I couldn't take much more of this woman and her lies. 'Denise Black won't stop making up lies up about me. She wants me out of her sight, and now she wants me in prison.' Tears were flowing down my cheeks, and it was becoming very difficult to make myself understood.

The doctor replied curtly, 'Quite frankly, my dear, that's not my problem.'

The policewoman was a little more sympathetic to me as I continued sniffling and started hyperventilating. She suggested that I calm down. My breathing was out of control. 'I can't take this anymore,' I sobbed. This was their cue to take me in. They tried several times to fingerprint me. In a way, the system was on my side, as the dabbing machine wasn't working properly. By this time my face was swollen, my eyes were blood-red and these officers *of the law* just kept taking pictures of me. Front. Side. Front again. Next on the scene was a man from the solicitors, he handed me his card and I took it. He said he was there to represent me. I looked at the card which read 'Reid and Black Solicitors'. I couldn't believe it, were they winding me up?

I became really paranoid, and even more tetchy and noisy. They sat me down in a small room. Just hearing the name *Black* was a trigger to escalate me to the next level of hysteria. I was surrounded by people with relatives and friends in high places. Was this another one of them? Was Black from 'Reid and Black Solicitors' part of the Denise Black clan?

Unbelievably, one of the first things the solicitor said was that we should have just moved house, rather than making complaints. I couldn't believe what I was hearing. 'They are going to keep you here all night,' he said, 'and in the morning you'll be going to court and straight to prison after that.'
I thought to myself - This solicitor is trying to put the fear of God into me and he's doing a pretty good job!

Mortified by what I was hearing, knowing this solicitor was supposed to be on my side, it was clear he was not acting in my best interests. I managed to leave the room, and went to the one person who seemed to have a grasp on the absurdity of the situation: Sgt Todd. He allowed me to call my sister who would arrange for my next solicitor, McIvor Farrell, to pay a visit. Amongst all this, despite having had the charges read out, I still didn't know specifically what I was being arrested for, what the actual offence was and then I was told that I had also given *the middle finger* to Denise Black. 'What? You cannot be serious.'

The policewoman led me to a cell, 'Oh we are serious all right.'

'You are putting me in a cell?' I questioned.

She nodded silently.

It was my worst nightmare, I was being treated as a criminal, surely I would wake up any second and realise it had all been a nasty dream and I would see the funny side of the joke the police were playing on me, locking me up for 'menacingly folding my arms and giving my neighbour the middle finger'. I have never used the middle finger in my entire life, that's when I realised the extent of Denise Black's dishonesty and false accusations.

On the way to the cell, I saw Tommy Mahood, a Police Inspector at Carrickfergus, behind the counter. He had come over to Antrim. Tommy used to hang around with me; he used to live next to my friend Brenda Donnelly, when we were 13 or 14 year-olds, meeting up at the Carrickfergus Leisure Centre. His face didn't crack when he saw me, and quickly found something else to do.

Suddenly my bladder was crying out to me, I was bursting for a *comfort break* and told the policewoman. 'There's one in the cell,' she said as she opened the door and pointed to the seatless, ceramic bowl in the corner of the cell. Puddles of urine surrounded the bottom of it. The smell in the cell was gut-wrenching, and worse, there was even a camera on high, aimed down at the seat, quite literally recording every movement.

'You surely don't expect me to use that?'

She shrugged her shoulders, closed the door on me, the crash echoing around the room. I stood for a moment, and then looked around, my jaw dropping away from my face in disbelief. I hobbled over to the bench, the only other piece of furniture in the room. I lay down and curled up into a foetal position on it. Again, I wanted to die.

Within 30 minutes, my claustrophobia kicked in again, and it felt like the cell was shrinking around me. I couldn't help myself, but I began to replay exactly where that fear had come from.

I now needed to go to the toilet really, really badly, but didn't want to be captured on tape doing so. A dilemma, but I simply wouldn't answer the call of nature while *big brother* was watching. My head was spinning and I felt like I was going to faint. I'd only had a few hours' sleep the night before and I had a touch of jet lag and travel weariness. The cell was creeping me out.

I had such a mixed bag of emotions going around in my head. Anger, hurt, frustration and rage. I was not in control. I started saying to myself - Breath in, breath out. I told myself - Calm the *feck* down, or you'll end up in a psychiatric ward. They'd love that.

From somewhere, I got the inclination to start singing. It might have sounded like madness to those outside the cell, but at least I wasn't that out-of-tune. For me, this was an act of self-preservation. And now I replayed, over and over, what had happened. I had made a statement of complaint about a neighbour harassing me. I had even noted I had two of my own witnesses. Not for the first time, Carrickfergus Police Station Northern Ireland (PSNI) was taking the neighbour's side. I had already suffered the trauma of two court appearances and my neighbour had had her victory. She, and her family and friends, had toasted with champagne on her driveway. But it wasn't enough. She was determined to break me, to send me to prison. Even the solicitor who was supposed to be representing me had told me that a jail cell was the eventual outcome, all because of this woman's obsession with bizarre fantasies.

I was locked up for several hours over those false allegations, even though there was not one iota of evidence to back up this woman's claims. It was only her word ... against mine … yet again.

It was my sister, who is in the police, who finally got me released. At that point, I found out I had been charged with the offense of giving Denise Black the middle finger, in front of her children.

I later found out that a good friend, Stephen, had picked Sophia up from the bus stop on that Friday afternoon. Stephen told her that I had been arrested and, understandably, Sophia was very distressed. Poor Stephen didn't stop to think what the reaction would be from Sophia to the threat of her mummy going to prison. Sometimes the truth has to be wrapped up for the sake of the damage it can cause.

9

Lie Detector

On 25 August 2008, during a police interview, I advised them I was going to get a lie detector test. A few days later, Sgt Steven Moore appeared at the door. Kevin had told him earlier not to bother dropping by when he had telephoned earlier, but Sgt Moore insisted stating he had to come out in our direction anyway. He made an excuse, something about a copy of a statement he wanted to leave for Kevin. When he arrived, Sgt Moore started up a conversation with Kevin about the Jet Ski on the driveway, and said one of his friends had one. Sgt Moore then revealed the actual reason he was there. He told me not to get a lie detector test, as they were considered a waste of money and you couldn't use them in court. I now know that is a lie, as they are admissible in court, subject to a judge's discretion.

I therefore asked lie detector expert Terry Mullins to fly over from England and administer a test on me. I confess, at the time, I was full of self-doubt and wondered if I was going crazy.
As I sat down with Terry I said I was so stressed and nervous. He told me it doesn't matter how stressed or nervous you are nerves don't affect the lie detector. (If you lie it will detect your faster heart rate, higher blood pressure and increased perspiration.)

He asked a serious of questions that I couldn't lie to, my name, my age, that sort of thing. Then the real questions started. He spoke softly in a monotone voice. Before each question he gave the dates that Denise Black had supplied to the police. 'Did you deliberately give the finger to your neighbour, Denise Black, in front of her children?'
'No.'
'Did you verbally abuse your neighbour?'
'No.'

'Did you witness Denise Black making verbal and threatening gestures towards you?'

'Yes.'

'Did you witness Denise Black standing with her hands on her hips making threatening gestures towards you?'

'Yes.'

I think there were about six questions in all. No more. After it was finished Terry sat for some time analysing the results. He told me that the test had used a Lafayette LX 4000 polygraph, as required by the US Polygraph Association. I shrugged my shoulders, 'And?'

'Your questions do not contain responses that are associated with deception.'

'Which means?'

He smiled, 'You are telling the truth Diane.'

I wanted to jump up and kiss him.

'On every question, you told the truth,' he said, 'even the one where you witnessed your neighbour making threatening gestures towards you and more importantly the question of did you give Denise Black the middle finger which resulted in the false arrest.'

The relief was enormous and instantaneous. I jumped up and gave him a hug. When he settled me down he gave me the results. Three pages of technical information which didn't make a lot of sense to me but on page two were the questions and alongside each question in big bold letters, NO DECEPTION DETECTED.

This test proved my innocence regarding all the false allegations. Not only did the lie detector test prove that I was telling the truth, it also demonstrated that Black herself was telling lies when she said she hadn't made threatening gestures towards me and pointed to her being the one who was harassing me! This lie detector test cost me £750, but it was worth every penny.

And yet the nightmare continued, despite telling the police about the lie detector and its results, I was taken to court every other month. They were fixated on the accusation that I had given the middle finger to Black in front of her children. I stood in front of judges and security personnel, treated like a criminal, only for the trial to be put off again and again. On one of these occasions, the prosecuting barrister declared, 'Your honour, we want to change the order from harassment to she's a pest.' I couldn't quite believe what I was hearing and how these people were treating me. Their cynical attitude to the law of the land was outrageous.

After six months, on 13 January 2009, my case went back to court, and they dropped all the charges against me. I was not even allowed to be present in court that time, I was simply told by my solicitor to go home, and I would be able to sue the police, PPS, Dr Haslam and Denise Black for making false allegations against me. Kevin noted that on the same day the charges were dropped, Mr Black turned up with a large white van, took all his furniture, emptied his house of all belongings and moved out. Denise Black never returned to the house after that day. Several days later a *For Sale or Rent* sign went up outside their house.

I did not hear from my solicitor for several weeks after that. When I eventually contacted him, he told me to get on with my life, he had decided against taking up my grievances. I contacted several solicitors after that to sue the system, and many solicitors promised me that they would take on my case. However, each time, within days, another set of doors would close on me and they would back down, refusing to press ahead with the case. Was this because I was fighting a corrupt system and Carrickfergus PSNI, the police themselves? Did they have a problem in that the system had been slated in the newspapers?

I believe the lie detector test and two witnesses saved me from prison. If it were not for that lie detector test, my daughter would have been without her mother for several months because of the lies Denise Black told. It's worth noting at this point that the appeal was audio recorded for three days and there was also a stenographer present in court. It's not the sort of material you'd expect to go missing.

10

The Plot Thickens

Dr Haslam was the doctor who didn't know me, but felt he had the power and capability to section me and have me confined in a mental hospital. I can't emphasise the disgust and contempt I have for this man and his actions, purely because his sister was involved in nothing more than a parking dispute with a neighbour, he felt compelled to attempt to ruin a life.

In September 2008, the GMC wrote out to the courts,

because of the misconduct allegations I'd made against Dr Haslam. The courts replied to the GMC and stated that they did not have recordings of any evidence. In order to release evidence of any kind through the courts, there had to be a request made to the Lord Chief Justice. Why were the transcripts of my three-day appeal so difficult to get hold of?

Since I started publicising my story in May 2011, I have received information from The Lord Chief Justice's office who confirmed that these transcripts exist. The GMC have now been informed of this new evidence, which they had previously been told did not exist. I am still waiting for some action to be taken.

Within a year of the newspaper story appearing in 2008, Dr Haslam sent the Sunday World a High Court Summons, stating he was suing them for defamation of character. He declared he didn't make the referral, but that it was Carrickfergus Police. I actually found this period of time, up until March 2011, the most stressful of my life. I still had a suspended sentence hanging over my head. I was still seeing Kevin's ex-neighbour Denise Black every other week.

Around the time the Sunday World had received the

writ from Dr Haslam, Denise Black saw me whilst I was out walking. It was at Seapark PSNI. She pulled up at the traffic lights and started to rant. She was in her car, had seen me out walking and drove past me. She was sitting at the traffic lights as I approached. She snarled like an animal and even though I had my headphones on, I could clearly see her mouthing words like 'fuck you, fuck this and that'. Her head was moving demonically, up and down, as it had done on many occasions before. She was sneering at me, her behaviour was very intimidating. That was enough for me. I couldn't believe she had fired all she'd loaded into her cannons against me and was still barking at me. I made a Statement of Complaint to Carrickfergus PSNI, who did nothing. I then complained to the Police Ombudsman, who also did nothing. They said there was no case to answer, because I had my headphones on, and could not hear what she was saying.

The writ from Dr Haslam to the Sunday World meant more pressure. Around this the time, I had started calling Ann Wilson, who was the head of CMHT in Carrickfergus. I was fretting because the police had stated they had made the referral, but Ann Wilson was telling me that under no circumstances can the police make such a referral. 'It has to be a doctor,' she said. She settled my nerves, but I must have driven her crazy. I rang her so many times; right up until the Sunday World went to court in March 2011.

I even met with the Sunday World's solicitor and barrister on a few occasions. They told me they were fighting this all the way to court, and there was nothing I should worry about. At some point all that changed, and the Sunday World folded like a pack of cards. They said, because of the risk factor, they would pay Dr Haslam a small amount of compensation and he wouldn't take it any further. 'What?' I said. 'You do know what he's done, or have you forgotten?' They said there was no real evidence, the police had said they had referred me to the CMHT, I told them that wasn't the case and that only a doctor had the power to do that.

'It couldn't have been the police, the CMHT wouldn't have listened to them,' I said.

And what was worse was that the police couldn't provide me with any evidence that they had referred me. The Sunday World kept telling me they had no proof that Dr Haslam had made the call and therefore they were paying him off. I thought this was completely bizarre behaviour, which beggared belief. It disgusted me.

11

Old Wounds Opened Up

I wanted it all to stop, honestly I did, and after many heated conversations with Kevin, we decided to let it lie and get on with our lives. Looking back on everything, the biggest cloud hanging over me, something that was never far away from my waking thoughts, was what Dr Haslam had tried to do to me. By far, that was the lowest blow of all and I was wracked with frustration that no solicitor was willing to take him on and hold him accountable for what was a serious breach of trust and abuse of his position.

I remember telling Kevin that even if he had just apologised and admitted he had made a mistake, it would have been some sort of closure and I would be able to get on with my life. I didn't want money, I didn't want to ruin the man, I just wanted him to acknowledge that what he had done had been a gross error of judgement. That was never going to happen. He had orchestrated a tissue of lies, claiming he had never referred me to any CMHT and that it must have been the police. So I had no option but to attempt to put it behind me and get on with life. At least what he had done was out in the open.

On 22 March 2011, a friend of mine sent me a press report that featured on the BBC News website stating that Dr Haslam of Dundonald Health Centre had been fully vindicated concerning the claims made in the Sunday World. I was distraught, my old wounds opened up as if someone had taken a tin opener to my brain. Enough was enough. I had tried to forget what this man had attempted to do to me but he had started all over again. He wasn't happy with the Sunday World settlement; he wanted to clear his name.

I wanted to get the full power of the law behind me in getting this nonsense retracted because that was not what the Sunday World had said, however, I was told by *legal eagles* that I would need between £10,000 and £15,000 to sue them. I didn't have that sort of money, so decided to try and sort it out myself. I telephoned the BBC and demanded they remove this untrue story from the website. Unfortunately, my direct approach failed.

Frustrated, and trying to work out how to make sure justice was done, I tried to meet with both the Director and Assistant Director of CMHT. Now, I had been relatively strong up to that point, but that press report, even if it was only on the internet, nearly tipped me over the edge. It appears the Sunday World and Dr Haslam came to a private arrangement on damages, due to an oversight made by the receptionist at CMHT Carrickfergus. The receptionist could not recall who she had taken the initial call from even though it should have been documented. You'll recall that it takes a doctor to refer someone to be sectioned and no doctor ever met me apart from Dr Haslam.

We managed to get a meeting with the Assistant Director of CMHT, It was as if she didn't have time for us, she was cold-hearted towards both Kevin and I. She just wasn't prepared to help us. I told her I was going to expose everyone involved in this debacle. She looked first at me, and then at Kevin, indignantly. She said if we continued with the action there would be *consequences*. What was she talking about? Were they planning to try and get me sectioned again?

That's when Marty McGartland began helping me out. Marty was a friend of a friend on Facebook and wasn't a great fan of the police. When his book, Fifty Dead Men Walking, was made into a movie in 2008, featuring Sir Ben Kingsley and Rose McGowan, it was a hit all over the world. He used to joke with me saying he should have retitled it Fifty Dead Men and a Woman Walking, just to ensure my case was recognised by the world. He helped by talking through things with me, discussing tactics, and suggesting how I could move things forward.

One of these exchanges led to me put into the public domain that I was demanding a meeting with the Director of CMHT. The exposure meant I finally got that meeting.

Initially, the Director appeared sympathetic. This all changed when I demanded a letter from him, stating that Dr Haslam made that referral. He blustered that we already had all the evidence. I pressed him on this, giving him proof that the BBC website, on 11 March 2011, had put on record that Dr Haslam had been fully vindicated. I wanted a signed and notarised letter after that date to prove to the public he hadn't been fully vindicated.

The Director stared coldly at me and spluttered that he didn't know if he could arrange a letter of that kind. He stood up, very slowly, and then looked down on me, before rhetorically enquiring, 'Do you know what's in your medical file?' I knew what he was getting at. This was going to be the exposure of my one time of self-harm. I was livid. He knew he had struck close to home and at that moment I categorically knew that someone at one point had shared that confidential information with Dr Haslam. 'Someone gave that information to Dr Haslam didn't they?' I questioned. He remained silent and, after several minutes of him repeating that he was unable to give me the letter I required, we left.

We continued to request the letter on both my website and Marty McGartland's. Marty also helped me out by highlighting my story on his Facebook page. Eventually, they caved in and many weeks later, the Director did send me an up-to-date letter, giving me exactly what I had demanded. He confirmed that Dr Haslam was not *fully vindicated*, as the BBC had originally said. Both the CMHT Press Office and I wrote to the BBC and demanded that these false press stories be removed. They ignored all communication. The *fully vindicated* article remains there to this day.

There was still an inappropriate referral made against me. To me, it seemed obvious that Dr Haslam was deeply involved in this referral. He was the only doctor that had met me, albeit briefly, and he never once divulged this information to the courts. At the appeal, Dr Haslam did not even have to answer any questions regarding this referral; the judge *gagged* me on asking him any questions about this.

When the GMC wrote to Dr Haslam about the misconduct allegations against him, he never once replied to them as to whether he had referred me or not. Surely, a simple 'no' would have sufficed? What did Dr Haslam have to hide, regarding the questions raised by the GMC? He is a disgrace to the profession, and I look forward to the day that the GMC agrees with me, and disbars him. I remained active in contacting various authorities as I tried to put Dr Haslam on the spot and urged him to come clean.

Then, a bolt out of the blue, from Oscar Donnelly, Director of Mental Health and Disability, Carrickfergus. The letter was dated 20 June 2011, addressed to me personally.

Paragraph three read:

'You were referred to our Community Mental Health Team by telephone on 25 August 2006. The CMHT record indicates that the referral was made by Dr Haslam.'

It was there in black and white … at last. It was as if someone had lifted a huge weight from me and what I had sincerely believed for five years had eventually been disclosed. The director went on to add that Dr Haslam disputed this but I didn't care. Their records showed otherwise. Their records proved that Dr Haslam was a liar. He had tried to cover this up for five years because he knew he had acted unlawfully and unethically. It was a closure of sorts and for the first time in a long while, I went to bed that night and slept like a baby.

It was thanks to Ian Puddick, a friend on social media from London, that I was able to get my story out. He was having his own problems with police corruption and was high profile at the time I contacted him. He put me on to Alex Geirns who was interviewing on police corruption on Edge TV. Ian was very kind to Sophia and I. He brought us over to the Edge studios and I was able to do a live TV interview while Ian was telling his own story. When

I was on air, the viewers were phoning in and were very angry, stating that a police officer cannot refer you to a CMHT. It clearly takes a doctor to make a referral and the only doctor to meet me was Dr Haslam.

Part Two

12

Moving On

It had been a nightmare, there was no other way to
describe it and yet, at last, I felt that I had been
vindicated and could move on with my life. I had to
for the sake of Sophia and Kevin. I had to rebuild my
life, to put it all behind me. The letter from the
director of the CMHT was a turning point for me
and, together with the results of the lie detector test,
at least I knew my sanity was intact.

I had contacted a few solicitors since the incident, hoping to sue Dr Haslam for what he had tried to do to me and although every single one of the solicitors agreed that I had a very strong case against him, each of them also stated that they would require substantial upfront payments of between £10,000 and £15,000 to take the case on and of course there were no guarantees. I discussed it with Kevin and we reluctantly agreed to let it lie. I had no confidence whatsoever in authority or the establishment. When I looked back at everything that had happened and how the police had backed Denise Black up, time and time again, we just knew that when it came to suing Dr Haslam and getting a fair hearing, we were up against it.

A couple of years later, we made another monumental decision and moved out of the house that had caused us so much pain and heartache. Despite Kevin's house being spacious and practical, I couldn't bear to walk out of his front door and look onto that house. I tried, but as soon as I set eyes on the front door it was as if a force field of negativity surrounded me and a cloud descended on me for the rest of the day. Despite the fact I may have had a great, positive, fulfilling day, as soon as I pulled into the street on an evening, that unshakable feeling of doom would return. I had to face facts, there was no way could I live in a street awash with poison. It would seep into my pores and eventually break me and I could feel it bringing me down on a daily basis. Kevin agreed to move into my house and make it our family home. So we packed up everything and moved, lock stock and barrel.

It was a new start and as soon as we had moved in together, I began to feel different. Each day I walked out of my front door I told myself it was a new day, the first day of the rest of my life and I consciously smiled as I walked into a street with nice, pleasant people, neighbours who wished me good morning, asked about Sophia, commented about the weather with a genuine, friendly smile on their faces.

There was a downside to living in my house, and that was that I had two police women as neighbours. I didn't know them; I had never met them or bumped into them in any of the police stations I had been to during my ordeal but they knew who I was. They wouldn't even look at me despite the fact I had wished them good morning several times. It didn't surprise me, it was one big clique and because of the negative publicity I'd brought to the force, they made it clear that they wanted nothing to do with me. I thought - No worries, I will keep myself to myself and get on with the rest of my life. At least that's what I told myself.

The reality was somewhat different, particularly when I slept. Despite trying to keep a positive mental attitude during daylight hours when out shopping or bumping into people in the street, behind closed doors, and especially when I went to bed in the evenings, it was as if my brain took on a whole new identity and the nightmares started.

I was back in the prison cell and the walls were closing in ... literally. The small scruffy bed would move as the walls inched ever closer to me and, at that point, I would wake up screaming, I'd be standing on the disgusting ceramic toilet, having no floor space to stand on, looking up towards the ceiling as that too inched towards me ready to crush me to death. I'd wake up in a cold sweat. I still couldn't believe they had put me in a cell over a parking dispute. I would tell myself - Get over it, get real and be positive, act normally and put it behind you. Easier said than done.

I had always enjoyed jogging around the streets, on the coastal paths and sometimes on the beach and it became a godsend to me. I started jogging more often and for longer periods, steadily building up the mileage. Whenever I was on my own at home and the negative thoughts or flashbacks started to hit me, I would reach for my running kit and head out the front door. Within a few minutes, as a light sheen of perspiration covered my brow, those thoughts would gradually fade away and, as the endorphins kicked in, I would get the buzz I loved so much. I'd think of how wonderful nature was and to hear the sound of the sea or the early morning birdsong as a new day dawned. I'd run in all weathers, it didn't bother me in the slightest, it was my escape and it became like a drug as I felt the fittest I had been since my teenage years.

Kevin's seafood business was flourishing and I took over running the orders and the accounts, I was his PA, but it didn't take over my whole working day. That suited me fine and by early or late afternoon I was generally finished and reaching for my running shoes.

One particular day I was late. It was about 8 pm but still light so I drove the car to Sloefield and set off along Shore Road. I had run no more than a mile or two when I looked up at the summer night sky, I could see that it was going to be a spectacular sunset, the sky was turning a deep crimson hue and I stepped up my pace. I felt good.

I didn't feel good for very long as all of a sudden I was thrown over head first onto the grass verge. Something had popped in my foot and excruciating pain was shooting through the area of my left ankle. It was as though someone had taken a dozen sharp knives and was thrusting them into my foot. I found myself squealing like a day old baby. I had fallen on my hands and knees and something told me not to move. I knew that it would be impossible to get up and spotted what looked like a mother and a daughter further down the street. I cried out, 'Help me please!' They didn't seem to be in any hurry as they looked at each other and shared a few words.

I stretched out my left leg and my ankle seemed to flop as another pain shot up my calf muscle. I lifted my knee and tried to steady myself by putting all of my weight on the right side in an attempt to stand. It was no good and I collapsed in a heap. I started to shake and a nauseous feeling washed over me. This was a serious injury. 'Help me, please,' I repeated. They eventually realised the seriousness of the situation and hurried over. Between the two of them, they lifted me to my feet but I wouldn't dare attempt to put any weight on my left ankle as I sensed that something was seriously wrong, something was broken, I was in no doubt. I thought I had perhaps stood on a brick or some other foreign object. As I looked towards the exact spot where I had gone down, I was dismayed to see a big dip in the pavement, at least three inches deep. There was a gap, a foot long, four feet wide and two inches deep. 'What the hell?' I mumbled to myself. No wonder I had fallen.

As I studied the pavement the tears rolled down my cheeks, I realised that it looked as if the council had been repairing the street lighting and that someone either hadn't finished the job or had got it seriously wrong. I cursed under my breath. The two women had flagged a passing car down. One of them said, 'We need to get you to a hospital this doesn't look good.' The other one told me I had turned grey and said that I looked awful. The driver had opened the door and as he saw me, he seemed a little reluctant to get involved.

'This girl needs to get to a hospital,' one woman shouted to him and the shock spurred him into action.

I don't know how but they bundled me into the car. If I thought the pain was bad lying on the pavement, it was nothing to what I was feeling as they manoeuvred me onto the front passenger seat of the car. My ankle had to be broken; there was no other explanation for the pain.

The driver was a young man in his late twenties and

I asked him to take me home so that Kevin could come to the hospital with me. I felt every bump, every stone as the man asked me 101 different questions. He asked me how I had fallen and where the pain was, and then he went on and on. 'So you think the pavement was faulty?'

'It was defective,' I replied, 'without a doubt.'

He seemed to be studying me.

'Don't I know you?' he asked.

'I don't think so.'

'Hmm, I'm sure your face is familiar.'

I didn't answer him, but my face had been plastered all over the Sunday World, so it wasn't uncommon that I was recognised occasionally. The questions continued.

'How big was the hole?'

'Big enough.'

'Was the tarmac loose?'

'Can't remember.'

'And there were no warning notices?'

I took a deep breath, 'Not that I noticed.'

I'd had enough. It was bad enough trying to control the pain without answering his constant questions. Then it dawned on me; he was questioning me like a policeman. I looked at the back of his head, close-cropped hair, forces style. He was fit looking, lean, a nice pressed shirt and his car was neat and tidy, spotlessly clean. Classic coppers car.

'Were there any contractors' signs nearby?'

'Thanks for the rescue but I'm in a lot of pain now and just breathing normally is an effort.'

He nodded, 'Sorry, it was just that …'

He didn't finish his sentence. 'Just what?' I quizzed.

'Oh, nothing … nothing at all.'

He shut up immediately and that convinced me he was a policeman because he knew exactly when to button his lip. He'd seen me in the Sunday World, or worse, my photograph had been circulated in the police stations of Northern Ireland. Perhaps I was the talk of the station with his colleagues in Carrickfergus Police Station. I was bad news, toxic, and this policeman knew exactly who I was. I was crying, I couldn't stop the tears and I could hardly breathe.

He pulled up outside my house and ran to my front door. I was relieved to see Kevin open the door and registered the shock on his face as the stranger relayed the story. Between them both they lifted me out of the car and put me into Kevin's car. At one stage the pain was so bad I was convinced I was about to pass out. As we drove away, I glanced back over my shoulder. My knight in shining armour had not moved his car and he had his mobile phone to his ear, speaking, with a very serious look on his face. I felt sick. On the way to Antrim Area Hospital, I explained what had happened. 'Where exactly?' Kevin asked. I looked up. We were on the Shore Road and no more than 200 yards from where I had tripped and fallen.

'Here, just along here,' I pointed.

Kevin slowed down.

'What are you doing? Take me to hospital,' I begged.

He stopped the car and put his hazard lights on. 'If that pavement caused your accident then we'll need a photograph.' He unbuckled his seat belt saying, 'I'll be quick. It looks as if the job is only half bloody finished. That footpath should have been cordoned off.'

Before we arrived at the hospital, I told Kevin about my rescuer, 'I'm convinced he was a copper, you should have heard the questions he was asking.'

Kevin laughed, 'The bloody irony of it - if a policeman has come to your rescue.'

'Not funny Kevin,' I muttered between the tears.

'It wouldn't surprise me Diane, there are a lot of coppers around here.'

Within 10 minutes, Kevin pulled up just outside emergencies. They brought me a wheelchair, pushed me into reception and settled me in the waiting area. A nurse took a quick look as I was waiting for a doctor. 'That's not good,' she said, 'I think you have ruptured your Achilles.' Within 20 minutes I sat in front of an older doctor who sent me for an x-ray.

He studied the results on the screen, turned to face me and smiled, 'No worries, it's just a bad sprain.'

Before I had a chance to question the seriousness of my injury, I was wheeled out into the main reception area and told that a nurse would attend to me soon. Another half an hour passed and a young Scottish nurse approached me. She took one look at my ankle, 'You'll be needing a plaster cast on that,' she said with a look of concern on her face.

I shook my head, 'I don't think so, the doctor said it was just sprained.'

She looked at me quizzically, 'Which doctor?'

As it happened, I looked up and the doctor was walking past us. 'Him,' I said.

She walked over to him, 'Doctor, can I have a word please?'

I caught snatches of their rather heated discussions. The nurse was not entirely convinced that it was just a sprain and I could hear her almost insisting on a plaster cast. The doctor was shaking his head, he was adamant it was just a sprain and even though the nurse asked for a second x-ray, the doctor refused. I heard him say it only needed an air cast, bandages and pain medication, 30/500 milligrams of Co-codamol. They put an air cast on me and sent me home with crutches.

13

A Return to The Scene Of The Crime

I spent an incredibly restless night, as did Kevin. He was up every two or three hours bringing me painkillers which worked for a while but I was popping so many, I think I was becoming immune. I would never have wished that night on my worst enemy. At around 7 am Kevin managed to prise me into a kitchen table seat and we sat drinking coffee.

Kevin was angry. He said the more he thought about the state of the pavement the more he thought the accident could have been avoided. Kevin was on a mission and just before 9 am, he left the house saying he was going to take some more photographs. He also wanted to make the foreman aware of the accident to prevent another one.

When he arrived, there was a squad of workers, working on the pavement and the street lighting on the opposite side of the road to where I had tripped. He sought out the foreman, explained what had happened the evening before and pointed to the spot. The foreman accompanied him and as Kevin approached the spot, he could see that it had been worked on. 'You've filled that in with cold tarmac out of a bag, within 12 hours of Diane falling in the hole,' Kevin said.

The foreman shook his head, denying it.

Kevin bent down, 'Yes you have. Look,' he pointed.

The tarmac wasn't even set properly and he disturbed it with his foot revealing the big hole that had caused my accident. He had the good sense to take another series of photographs. It would be one of the best decisions he would ever make. These were before and after shots, and the fact they had filled in the holes so quickly would be proof that the contractors were admitting that they hadn't completed the job correctly in the first place.

'What are you doing?' the foreman asked.

Kevin told him that he had taken photographs just after the accident and now he had evidence of the repair that should have been done at the time. As Kevin walked away the foreman was demanding to see the photographs but Kevin refused. He returned home even angrier than when he had left. He said that the accident should never have happened; it could have and should have been prevented if someone had done their job properly.

The experience of what Hell may be like is sometimes over-exaggerated. *I've been to Hell and back* is an expression that is used far too often but, believe me, the next 10 days of suffering in the house was an experience I would never wish anyone to go through and I am sure that the Devil himself couldn't have made me suffer more. Day after day I convinced myself that it would start to improve, that it was just a matter of time and before long I would be walking normally. In a matter of months, I would be running again. Running was my drug, I needed it like oxygen, and yet after nearly two weeks I still couldn't put my foot on the floor, let alone put any weight on it.

From day to day I was walking around the room holding onto furniture and conscious that I was more or less just hopping around the house on one foot. I was now concerned because of the pain I was getting in my right hip. I knew what the cause was, the whole right side of my body was trying to over compensate for the fact that the left side was useless. And that's how I felt … completely useless. I Googled my injury. What exactly was the Achilles tendon? It was the biggest tendon in the body, stretching from the bone of your heel to your calf muscle, like a big springy band of tissue at the back of your ankle just above your heel. It's the tendon that allows you to point your toes toward the floor and raise yourself on your tiptoes. It wasn't common for the Achilles tendon to get injured. 'It can be a mild tear,' I read. The pain sometimes described as 'moderate' but, if the pain is 'severe', the Achilles tendon may be partly torn or completely ruptured. 'This is bad news,' it said. I read with dismay, 'If you have any of these symptoms and think you've ruptured your Achilles tendon, you should see a doctor urgently. An Achilles tendon needs treating straight away, if you cannot get to your GP immediately, you should go to accident and emergency at your nearest hospital. An untreated Achilles rupture can result in permanent disability.'

Just reading those last few words filled with me with dread. I told Kevin that he had to take me to the hospital that day, I was now seriously concerned. I could take the pain, I had quite a high tolerance for it, but I wanted to run again and the thought of not being able to get out on the streets was more than I could dare to imagine.

As he had done for two weeks, Kevin acted as my crutch and I hobbled towards the car. He dropped me off at the entrance to the hospital, went to park up as I sat on a seat outside and within 10 minutes we were walking (I was hobbling) into emergencies. Coincidently, as I looked up, I saw the same doctor who was on duty when I'd had the accident and as soon as he saw me hopping through emergencies his face fell. But he couldn't avoid us and walked over, staring at my leg. 'Not good,' he said, as he looked at his watch, then told Kevin and me to go for a bite to eat in the cafeteria and he would try to sort out an ultrasound.

Within the hour I had been called to a treatment room. Two nurses were attending to me and I must say I wasn't inspired with confidence. I tried my best not to gravitate towards paranoia, but with everything that had happened to me at the hands of the police, the courts, Dr Haslam and numerous solicitors; I couldn't help feeling a sense of déjà vu. Were these two nurses as clumsy and incapable as they were making out or was it all a deliberate act? They seemed to sense where the problem was, the Achilles tendon, and started to apply a gel as they applied the ultrasound. They kept asking me what the doctor had said originally. I repeated several times that the doctor had said it was a bad sprain. 'Ah well,' one of them said, 'the doctor is always right.' I looked over at Kevin and he gave me a look that said – 'don't say anything'.

We waited for the result of the ultrasound. Kevin reassured me that the scan would pinpoint the cause of the problem, which would result in treatment, a cast, an operation or whatever and that within a few months I would be starting my first training run. It was a comforting thought as I looked at the clock on the wall and then my watch and then the time display on my mobile phone. Eventually, the two nurses returned. 'Nothing wrong with the Achilles,' was the first thing she said. 'Just a sprain as the doctor said.' She asked me to come through to the treatment room and told me she would bandage it. I felt like crying. Why was nobody listening to me? Why on earth would I be hobbling around like this after two weeks if I had just sprained my ankle?
I said to her, 'Surely this is more than just a sprain nurse?'
'The doctor is always right.'

'But I've had sprains before as a teenager on the sports field and they all started to improve after 24 hours. I can assure you nurse, that this is nothing like a sprain, I have a serious injury and it's not getting any better.'

She unwrapped the packaging of the bandage. 'Sure, but we are all getting a little older and the older we get the longer injuries take to heal.'

'I accept that, but I'm not a pensioner, there is something seriously wrong with my Achilles tendon. I can almost pinpoint exactly where the problem is and it's nothing to do with the joints or the bones of my ankle.'

She looked up as she started to apply the bandage saying, 'Doctor will be with you soon.' Then with a little smirk, 'The doctor is always right.'

What happened next was bizarre, something to this day I can't explain away. The doctor walked into the treatment room about 15 minutes after the nurse had gone. He checked over the strapping, seemed quite happy with the way it had been applied. 'Feeling better?' he asked.

'No, not at all doctor, I'm no better than when I came to see you two weeks ago.'

He raised an eyebrow and looked at me, 'Is there anything else you want to tell me?'

'Sorry?'

'Is there anything else you want to tell me?' he repeated.

Was he suggesting that he knew my Achilles was damaged? And did he know that I knew and that he was at fault and fishing for more information?

'Well,' I said, 'I'm a bit concerned that nothing has shown up on the ultrasound.'

'In what way?'

'My Achilles tendon, something should have shown up on the ultrasound.'

He sighed, 'There's nothing wrong with your Achilles tendon, Mrs Taylor, and it's just a sprain.'

Before I could answer him, he was on his feet and walking away towards the door. He didn't even turn to face me as he called out that he would sort out a physiotherapist and authorise some more pain medication. And then he was gone. I shook my head and looked at Kevin. He buried his face in his hands.

I was so low that evening. I sat with my foot up. With the new bandage my foot pulsed and throbbed and Kevin brought me painkillers every four hours. As I hobbled up the stairs around midnight, I tried to tell myself that the next day would be different, that I would wake up and see a little, but noticeable, improvement. It wasn't much to ask.

14

Physiotherapy and Strange Goings On

I started two months of physiotherapy, courtesy of our National Health Service (NHS). On the morning I arrived at Carrickfergus Health Centre, I tried to remain positive. The two hospitals, (Antrim Area Hospital and Carrickfergus Health Centre) had been corresponding with each other, so I looked forward to someone at least telling me that I had a serious injury to my Achilles tendon, but more importantly, the type of treatment needed to put me back on the mend. This was all I wanted, at this stage I didn't want to blame any doctors or nurses, mistakes could be made and I'd read in the past that even broken bones can be missed on x-rays. I assumed a tear in a tendon was far harder to spot. What I couldn't quite accept, however, was that I had hobbled into a hospital two weeks after being told I'd sprained an ankle and, despite almost pleading with the staff that I had some sort of rupture of the Achilles tendon, they sent me home again with a 'Doctor knows best' flea in my ear.

The physiotherapy treatment consisted of rubbing the area of my Achilles tendon at the back of my heel. When the physiotherapist appeared to concentrate on this particular area, I breathed a sigh of relief. At last, it appeared that someone had pinpointed the exact area of the injury and even though the physiotherapist took me to the point of agony at times, she assured me that I would start to regain movement and flexibility and I would eventually return to normal. 'I'm so pleased,' I told the young woman in her early 20s, 'that someone has accepted I have a serious injury to my Achilles tendon, they tried to tell me I had a sprained ankle.' This is when everything started to become very strange.

At this point, I expected the physiotherapist to open up some sort of dialogue with me, tell me what she was doing and the type of things she would be putting in place. She was working on my Achilles tendon, which was as clear as day, and I naturally expected her to come back with some sort of response that this was no sprain, it was a rupture of the Achilles tendon. She said nothing. She didn't even nod her head.

I had an appointment every two weeks on average. Every appointment was the same. A severe, almost aggressive, very painful massage on the area just above my heel to the extent that it started to bruise. She was quite happy to discuss this and assured me it was normal. 'Normal for a ruptured Achilles tendon?' I asked. She remained silent, not once did she mention a ruptured or damaged Achilles tendon, she referred to it as the *damaged area of the ankle*.

I must confess that after she had massaged the *damaged area of my ankle* at each session there was a little more movement in the ankle and at first, I dared to believe that the treatment was working. Sadly, it wasn't to be. A few hours after each treatment session, my ankle was more or less back to having very little movement and severely painful if I attempted to put any weight on it.

I was loading up on painkillers every four hours and the pain woke me at least once or twice a night. When it did, the routine was always the same; there was a glass of water and a bottle of pills by my bed. I'd take two and lay my head back on the pillow. About an hour later the pain would begin to ease and about another hour later I'd drift off to sleep. It was around this time that nature started to adapt to my injury. Although there was no real movement in my foot, I was able to put a little weight on it. Kevin was optimistic, he said that a little improvement each day meant that I was *on the mend*. I knew differently.

A good friend told me that I needed to claim for Disability Living Allowance (DLA) because I could no longer walk properly and my ability to work had been severely impaired. She said it was all quite simple, after filling in a few forms they would contact my doctor who would confirm my current medical condition. I went online to check it out, it all looked fairly straightforward. 'Disability Living Allowance (DLA) is money for people who have extra care needs or mobility needs (difficulty getting around) as a result of a disability.' It told me about the lower, mid, and higher weekly benefit, the higher benefit could even assist with the purchase of a car. If nothing else, even the lower level of payment might help with taxis so that I didn't need to burden Sophia and Kevin 24 hours a day.

I filled in the forms and made an appointment with my then doctor, Dr Crothers, just to tell her that I had applied and that they would be writing to her. She said that there was nothing to worry about, it was just a formality. She carried out a brief examination and while she didn't confirm that I would qualify for DLA, she said that DLA had been brought out for people exactly like me. Her letter would confirm my disability, the fact I was immobile and needed constant support and that I was unable to carry out normal work. She would also document my chronic pain and the medication I was permanently on. I thanked her for her time and left.

Several weeks later I received a reply from the Department for Work and Pensions (DWP). The letter told me that my claim had been assessed at the lower level and I would receive a payment of around £23 per week. It said at the bottom of the half-page letter that I hadn't amassed sufficient points to take me above the lower level.

15

Coping... Just

My body was strangely coping with the damage. It was as if my whole body had changed and subconsciously, I learned to walk in such a way that I was able to take a short step with my right foot and a smaller step with my left, while distributing my weight to my right side. I couldn't move quickly but at least I could move on level, even and firm ground. Walking on an uneven surface was still impossible and soft grass or sand was out of the question. Kevin said that perhaps the physiotherapy was working. It wasn't, it was my built-in determination that I somehow had to get on with it. And yet in the back of my mind, I knew I wasn't doing myself any long-term favours.

Pain is nature's warning signal; it tells us that a particular area of our body is being damaged. It is as simple as that. The pain is speaking to us, telling us that we either need the problem rectified, or we need to make adjustments to heal the damage and prevent it from happening again or getting worse. I knew that my ruptured tendon should have been treated within just a few hours of the accident. It wasn't treated. I now have inoperable scar tissue because it wasn't treated, they left it too late. At that time, my body was readjusting and learning to cope. It was healing the damage as best as it could.

I was learning to live with chronic (long term) pain. It's a medical fact if someone walked into a doctor's surgery with a bad injury and the doctor asked them what the pain level was on a scale of 1-10 and the accident had happened a few hours earlier, they would likely measure the pain level around an 8 or a 9. Consequently, a person who has been dealing with a chronic problem for many months may describe the pain level as a 4 or a 5 even though, clinically, they were experiencing a much worse *injury* situation than the person claiming to be an 8 or a 9 and would have probably sustained much more damage to their body.

This is exactly where I was, and to make matters worse I was swallowing painkillers like Smarties, which put my pain level at around 4 or 5. I tried to walk as normally as I could, forcing myself to at least try and put my foot on the ground yet knowing that the long term implications were going to be severe.

Around this time, Kevin had walked the pavements where I had had my accident. He noticed that the area that the contractors had been working on (where I had the fall) had been repaired. He had been in construction for some years and knew a little bit about reconstructing pavements after repairs. However, on other parts of the road, where the pavements were maintained by the council, he noticed similar levels of disrepair and contacted the council to inform them. He explained about my accident and said although he knew that the contractors were responsible, he wanted to warn the council, otherwise, there would be another accident before too long.

We now knew that my injury wasn't going to heal up any time soon and we dared to talk about the possibility that my disability may be prolonged … long term. It was a depressing thought but we had to face facts. I was severely impaired and restricted in my movements. My daily routine had changed beyond all recognition. Kevin suggested we contact a solicitor as clearly someone was at fault. What if the worst came to the worst and it impacted on my general health, my ability to work and live a normal life?

We contacted a solicitors' office, McIvor Farrell, and presented them with the facts. They were hot on the case and within a couple of weeks one of their solicitors, Conor Woods, arranged to meet Kevin and me at the scene of the accident. He brought what I can only describe as a small gang of men, some in *hivis* jackets, some in suits, representatives of the local council, the contractors and an insurance company. Conor Woods was almost purring when Kevin showed him the before and after photographs. He said something about an open and shut case, described the photographs as 'dynamite' and said that the firm (contractor) was clearly to blame and their insurance company would have no alternative but to pay up. While Conor Woods was smiling, like that cat that got the cream, I wanted nothing more than someone to treat me and put me right, to get me back to normal sooner rather than later. As we drove away, I stared out of the car window wishing that I could have turned back the clock, perhaps either not going for a run that day or taking an alternative route.

While the physiotherapist was undertaking work on the *damaged area of the ankle*, this didn't appear to be giving me any more movement. She also did work on my hips and back, pointing out that as a result of the *damaged area of my ankle*, my whole body had suffered. She said that the entire area of my back and hips were unnaturally out of line as if someone had twisted me as far as they could and left me in the same position. Didn't I know it? I was in a mess. I had aged at least 10 years as far as my physical condition was concerned and all I wanted was for someone to put me right. She worked a lot on my right hip with an electronic machine and was more than happy to talk technically about hips, ligaments and joints. Just don't ask her to discuss ruptured Achilles tendons; that was something she didn't want to address.

Halfway through the treatment, the physiotherapist mentioned the possibility of gait analysis via a Gait Machine. She explained that gait analysis tested the exact movement patterns of an individual as they walked or their *gait*. She said the machine was quite common in running shoe stores. A sort of treadmill, where the machine takes the results of the body's movements, patterns and behaviours, designed to fit the individual with tailor-made running shoes, specifically for each foot. It was quite common for an individual to have a leg length discrepancy, and the top sports shops, after analysing the Gait Machine data, could recommend running shoes with built-in heels to compensate for one leg being shorter than the other.

I asked her what that had to do with my condition. She hesitated. I got the impression that she was very careful in what she was saying but she admitted at last, that there was an issue with my foot and mentioned that a *gait analysis* may pinpoint the problem and, as a result of the data capture, may recommend heel inserts which could rectify the injury in the long term. It was the first piece of positive news Kevin and I had heard since the accident. While we left then with a degree of optimism, on our next few visits to the physiotherapist, we asked about the Gait Machine analysis but never got a clear answer nor did we get an appointment with the Belfast Health Trust. In the end, we gave up asking.

I had seven or eight sessions with the physiotherapist

from Carrickfergus and although I think I saw an improvement in the flexibility of my back and hip, my foot, the *damaged area of the ankle,* clearly wasn't getting any better. It was a worrying time. By now Kevin and I had studied and researched my injury, where the pain was and the extent of the damage. We were in no doubt that I had seriously ruptured my Achilles tendon and my leg should have been immobilised and put in a plaster cast from day one. We talked to friends in the medical profession, friends of friends and some family too, and in our minds, there was no doubt. We even Googled specialist websites for Achilles trauma. The overriding consensus was that any rupture to the Achilles tendon should be treated initially with immobilisation so that the foot could not move at all. The tendon would knit back together naturally and then, and only then, physiotherapy could begin to bring back flexibility and movement.

I felt that I'd been patient but it wasn't working. I couldn't shake the feeling that my body had somehow accepted the disability and the muscles around the injury were adapting to cope. I feared that this injury, the pain and the immobility would be with me for the rest of my life. I sank into a depression. I just wanted someone to put me right. But first of all, they would need to come clean, admit that they had misdiagnosed my injury and then perhaps we could get started. I recall talking with Kevin one evening. He analysed it perfectly. He said that nobody in the Belfast Health Trust was prepared to admit the oversight. They had all pulled together, closed ranks - doctors, nurses, radiologists and physiotherapists. Not one of them was prepared to utter the words 'ruptured Achilles tendon' or 'sorry' or 'we made a mistake' even although it was as clear as day that they had.

16

That Sinking Feeling

The word vulnerable always comes to mind. I was disabled, there was no other word to describe my lack of mobility and it frightened me. I had an overwhelming fear of being attacked and not being able to run away. I addressed the way I was feeling and put it down to the attacks I'd suffered in the past. Getting trapped in the car at Toomebridge and beaten by the girls was bad enough, yet always in the back of my mind, I knew that if I could have made it out of the car I was fast enough and strong enough to get away. It was the fight or flight mentality of nature and I was never one to stay and fight because, for me, running was always the better option and I was good at it. Some instances from the past frightened me; the man masturbating in his car was seriously disturbing for me because I didn't know what his next move was going to be. He could have decided to open the door and drag me in. As much as it had scared the hell out of me, I hadn't felt particularly vulnerable because I had been strong and fit and was able to run quicker than the average man in the street and for far longer. Not anymore.

My physical health was poor and my mental health was going downhill fast because everything that kept me sane had been snatched away from me. Not only was I unable to run, but also I couldn't go to the gym, kick box, or even go for a decent walk. I stayed indoors and never went out on my own. I just couldn't face it and I knew that it put an additional strain on Kevin and Sophia. Between them, they walked the dogs, shopped and cleaned the house. I struggled to cook, wash the dishes and even standing in one place for a prolonged period was a severe effort.

It was a rough period of my life and the hope of getting better and recovering the mobility I'd had prior to the accident was slowly slipping away. I also noticed that the bubbly, always positive attitude was something of a distant memory. I started having nightmares. I was old and in a wheelchair or walking deformed like an old cripple with a walking stick. And when I did wake up I didn't want to get out of bed again because I knew that as soon as I put my foot on the floor, the pains would start, the pain in my foot, in my calf muscles, my thighs, my hips and my lower back. I just wanted to stay in bed the whole day. I started to realise that perhaps my subconscious mind was trying to tell me something. There was no happy ending, no get out of jail free card or a miracle operation. This was it. I was disabled … for life.

We had several meetings with our solicitors over the next few weeks. They detailed the amount of my claim. It included, amongst other things, loss of earnings, the necessary domestic services, footwear requirements, adaption of the house, future care and attention and travel and transport. The figure they were talking about was around £250,000. It was a drop in the ocean; I was disappointed because I knew it reality that the amount they had come up with wouldn't be the amount I would receive. The amount was up for negotiation and there would be a lot of discussions and arguments in court and then, of course, the solicitors would want their cut. I sank deeper into a depression. A human being can survive anything if there's light at the end of the tunnel. It's when you can't see the end of that tunnel, that shining light that pulls you on and encourages you just a little no matter how small, that you begin to give up hope.

I had decided that the physiotherapy was doing my ankle no good, Kevin said, 'Enough is enough.' We made another appointment with a doctor at Greenisland Health Centre. I believed that if he saw my lack of movement and the way I limped into his surgery, he would have no option but to refer me to someone (although I didn't know who) who could help me. My ankle was now so stiff and restricted in movement, that I was convinced it was necessary to have some sort of surgery.

As Kevin and I walked into the doctor's surgery, he could have been under no illusion that I was in a bad way and I could see it in the expression on his face. The situation was taking its toll on Kevin, a disability does not just affect the individual, it affects the whole family. Kevin sat down in the seat alongside me and we began to relay the events of the past few months. Kevin, described the accident and our subsequent visit to the emergency department at the hospital. He was quite blunt in his analysis of the situation, he put the blame fairly and squarely on the Belfast Health Trust. He categorically stated that, in his opinion, they failed to diagnose or treat a very serious injury and for many weeks passed it off as nothing more than a sprained ankle. The doctor started to get defensive.

Kevin stood his ground. He pointed to my ankle, 'It's clearly more serious than a sprain, doctor, you've seen how she walked in and it's been over three months since the accident. She needs an MRI scan.' It happened again. The doctor took a deep breath, shook his head, told me and Kevin that his colleagues within Belfast Health Trust were consummate professionals, well trained medical men and women and he wouldn't have a word said against them.
'So, are you telling me this is a sprained ankle?' I asked.

I had simply pointed out the obvious but the doctor wouldn't have it, he wouldn't have a word said against any of the doctors or nurses who worked for the Belfast Health Trust. I'm ashamed to admit we had some cross words. I was on the verge of tears because, once again, I had dared to believe that by seeking yet another medical opinion, somebody would wave a magic wand and the real treatment necessary for my recuperation would begin. That was all I asked. I didn't care about the mistakes that had been made, the past was the past and all I wanted to do was to look forward to the future in the hope that I would regain the movement in my foot which would enable me to walk, do normal household chores, cook, take the dogs out and eventually run again.

Kevin was getting animated, 'Well who should we blame?' he asked the doctor. 'They messed it up from the start.'

The doctor was wagging his finger at Kevin, I'll never forget his words as his voice crept up a decibel, 'Don't you be slating the Belfast Health Trust, I won't have it.'

Kevin was getting even more upset as the doctor asked me to walk in front of him. I walked up and down the surgery. The doctor agreed it didn't look right.

'Is it painful when you walk?' he asked.

'Excruciatingly so,' I replied.

Both Kevin and I caught the look. He didn't believe me.

'It's worse when she takes her shoes off and walks in bare feet,' Kevin said. He looked at me, 'Take your shoes off Diane. Show the doctor.'

The doctor tried to say there was no need but I was already pulling my shoes off. Kevin was right. My shoes gave me a little support and, with a heel, I could walk and put a little weight onto the ankle. Walking in bare feet was when it really affected me and showed the full extent of my disability. Before the doctor could object any more, I had my shoes off and took a few paces towards his desk. My whole body subconsciously lurched over to the right as I started to walk. Then, as the doctor studied my motion, a different look in his eyes as he saw the obvious gap between my heel and the floor as he realised how much pain and discomfort I was in and that it was impossible for me to put my left foot flat onto the floor.

After leaving the doctor's surgery, we were both quite distressed. I was having a go at Kevin for sticking to his guns and getting quite animated but deep down I admired his resolve and sympathised with his frustration. Kevin wanted the same thing as me; my mobility back. Yet with every door we opened we met a brick wall of silence and dare I say, mystery. What was their problem? Why couldn't they just come out and say that a mistake had happened and that they were going to sort me out? Better late than never.

After physiotherapy stopped, I was referred to the Integrated Clinical Assessment and Treatment Service (ICATS) which was founded to help orthopaedic patients get the most appropriate treatment. By that time, it was more than six months after the initial accident. At first, I was a little reluctant to go, but I discussed this with Kevin. It couldn't do any harm. As I read the pamphlet it mentioned assessing patients for possible surgery, bringing together expertise from musculoskeletal teams who would provide specialist assessments and advice. I was referred to the Musgrave Park Hospital, Orthopaedic Triage Service and I was assessed by ICATS. During the first consultation with ICATS, they recommended an MRI scan. They said they would send a letter out to me as soon as possible. I received the letter and was given a date for my MRI scan within a week. Little did I know the secrecy and mystery was about to jump up to another extraordinary level.

I attended the MRI scan, was put through the machine and told that the results may take several weeks. Sure enough, some weeks later a letter came in the post asking us to attend an appointment. The results were analysed by a very nice, young, female doctor. And then she said, and I quote word for word, 'Nothing has shown up on the MRI scan, but we are going to refer you to a surgeon.' Kevin looked at me and shrugged his shoulders.

I looked at the doctor and said, 'But doctor, how can the results be normal? I'm in terrible pain and I have no mobility, you've seen how I walk.'

She didn't answer.

'If the results are normal, then why are you referring me to a surgeon? What is he going to do?'

'It's just routine,' she said.

It didn't make any sense at all.

We left the hospital no further forward, and on the drive back home we decided it was time to get a second opinion from someone outside the remit of the Belfast Health Trust.

17

More Opinions

I went privately, to a doctor from Ulster Independent, Mr Alistair Wilson. I explained the situation, took him through everything that had happened, from the initial accident, diagnosis and the treatment (or lack of) thereafter. He listened patiently and took everything in. He made me walk across his treatment room many times. He was very quiet. I expected him to say that the Achilles tendon had been ruptured at some point but he didn't, he said very little. Eventually, he told me that I needed steroid injections, two of them. 'They will take away the inflammation around the ankle, improve the pain levels and help your flexibility.'

I dared to believe. I asked him what the success ratio was. He spoke positively, said he had suggested steroid injections for many patients and the results were good.

'If they work, is there the possibility that I could even run again?'

He nodded. 'Quite possibly,' he said.

The positivity and expectation I felt leaving his practice quickly disappeared when I started to research the steroid injections. The doctor hadn't told me about the failure implications, that the steroid injections could severely damage the Achilles tendon and make it worse. I read one expert's concerns that as a result, the steroids can cause a *cheese string* affect to the tendon and cause side effects too.

Within three or four days, after discussing it over with Kevin and taking some more advice, we both concluded that it wasn't worth the risk. I was determined that I wouldn't let anyone talk me round. That was until I talked to my solicitor, Conor Woods and he dropped a bombshell. 'You have to go through with the steroid injections because you have to demonstrate to the insurance company that you have explored every alternative to regain your health and mobility.'

'But they are bad news, I've read a … '

He held up his hand and stopped me dead. 'Diane, a highly respected doctor has recommended steroid injections.'

'But … '

'But nothing. Can you imagine getting to court and they find out you have refused treatment? We won't have a cat in Hell's chance of getting you the settlement you deserve. You need to keep the appointment with the surgeon, Mr Wilson. We need you to follow through with his advice too.'

Against my better judgement, I went for the steroid injections at Musgrave Park Hospital that Alistair Wilson had recommended. When I got to the hospital, I was greeted by a tall handsome doctor, Dr Taylor. He joked and asked if we were anyway related in any way. He asked me about my pain levels. I said my pain levels were quite high that day, around 8 or 9. He asked what I was expecting from the injections. I said I was hoping that I would be able to run soon after. He looked at me like I had 10 heads. He said, 'Where did you get that information from?'

I said, 'Mr Wilson told me that I could possibly run

after having them.'

He replied, 'The steroid injections will reduce the inflammation and help with the chronic pain but nothing more than that.'

He gave me a double dose. Even as they entered my system I knew that I had made a grave error in agreeing with the surgeon. While they initially took away the inflammation, the side effects were horrendous. Almost immediately I suffered from hot flushes and I became agitated. They made no difference to the flexibility in my foot and I still had no dorsiflex movement.

I can't describe my appointment with the orthopaedic surgeon at Musgrave Park Hospital, Mr Gary Colleary in any other terms than an unpleasant ordeal. From the first time I met him, there were dark vibes and it was clear from the start that he looked upon me as nothing more than an annoyance. He seemed very agitated from the moment I walked into his surgery. He had no time for me, he made me feel like a nuisance, a pest, but, more than that, he made me feel as if I was faking the injury.

He started by asking me to walk across the room. After I had completed a couple of circuits, he took some notes and then asked me to remove my shoes. I dreaded taking them off because there was a huge difference in my posture and ability to walk in bare feet. He told me to walk across the room. I took a deep breath and started to limp across the room. At first, he appeared to study the way I walked. Then he spoke, 'Put your foot flat on the floor.'

I looked up, 'I can't doctor.'

'Yes you can, put your heel on the floor.'

'Believe me doctor,' I said, 'nothing would give me greater pleasure than to be able to put my foot flat on the floor because that would mean I would be able to walk correctly.'

He raised his voice, 'Just put it flat.'

'I can't.'

'Yes, you can.'

I pointed down at my heel, 'That's as far as I can go, it won't go any further.'

So he sulked. He took a deep breath and sighed in an obvious act of petulance and frustration. 'Very well, sit down on the seat.'

'There's no need to shout,' I said. 'Believe me doctor, I'm a lot more frustrated than you are because I've been trying to put my foot flat for over eight months now.'

He moved around in front of me and took a hold of the ball of my foot with his left hand while his right hand cupped the back of my ankle, the palm of his hand resting on the Achilles tendon area at the heel. He told me to relax as much as I could. I took a deep breath and breathed out.

'Relax your foot.'

'It is relaxed doctor.'

'It's not, it's stiff and rigid.'

'Yes doctor, that's what I have been saying for eight months.'

He didn't give up immediately. I got the distinct impression that he sincerely believed that I was somehow stiffening my foot deliberately. He twisted my foot back and forth, then tested my good foot for flexibility and kept alternating between the two as if trying to catch me out. After a few minutes, he had no option but to accept that I was telling the truth, that the movement in my damaged ankle was minimal. I wanted him to apologise because it had been clear to me that he thought I was faking it. I didn't ask him for an apology and none was forthcoming, but I sensed that the penny had dropped. He now knew that my ankle was as bad as I had tried to tell him from the beginning. I sat while he made a few notes. He said he was going to refer me to a physiotherapist. I told him I'd already had eight sessions for physiotherapy which left my Achilles black and blue and it didn't help. He said, 'There's physio and then there's physio here at Musgrave Park Hospital.'

The physiotherapist was called Ingrid. We visited Ingrid 12 times in all, Kevin was with me the first two times. At the first appointment, she stated midway through the session, 'You have clearly damaged your Achilles tendon.'

The following week, when I mentioned my damaged Achilles tendon, she completely backtracked, she said, 'It's not your Achilles after all.'

'But you worked on the area of my Achilles tendon last week, so how can it not be damaged?'

'You took a machine to the exact area,' Kevin said.

She explained she had been giving nothing more than a massage. When Kevin questioned her some more she simply closed up saying, 'It's just tight because of damage to the ligaments. Nothing more than that Diane.'

For several weeks Ingrid gave me acupuncture for my ligaments and the Achilles area. She gave me sessions where my right foot was pushing a weight-bearing machine but when it came to my left foot it was shaking. She would slap my leg and say, 'Stop!' She got me to walk barefoot with my hands on my hips like being on a catwalk and said, 'You're wobbling like a little rag doll.' Afterwards, I would be in excruciating pain for weeks. The mystery was deepening.

However, during the final visit with Ingrid, after 12 sessions, she said she couldn't help me anymore as I was seriously injured. When she signed me back into the care of Gary Colleary, she recommended treatment to manage my chronic pain, my ankle, knees and my hips. We discussed the possibility of another letter from Dr Crothers to the DLA in the hope of increasing my DLA mobility which could result in the purchase of a car. She said she would be writing to Gary Colleary with full details of the treatment I had received and the extent of my mobility and chronic pain.

There was another referral, this time with Mr Andrews FRCS. Kevin had come to the appointment with me this time and Mr Andrews had an x-ray up on the screen. He was pointing out areas of the deltoid ligaments and the dark areas which signified scarring, attributed to the injury. Kevin noticed something and stood up. He walked a little closer to the machine and pointed to my Achilles tendon, just above the heel. 'And here doctor,' Kevin said, 'this dark area too, this looks like scarring.'

Mr Andrews nodded, 'Yes, I believe so, a little bit of scar tissue around the Achilles tendon.'

He switched the machine off quickly and told us the report would be ready soon. I thought that was rather abrupt and he seemed in a hurry to get us out of the office because it became apparent that he didn't want to mention any scarring on the Achilles tendon. Mr Andrew's report confirmed the injury to my ankle, that I walked with an 'antalgic gait' (walking lopsided against pain) and there was evidence of chronic regional pain syndrome but there was no mention of any Achilles scarring. Kevin and I thought that was rather strange.

I was referred to another orthopaedic surgeon by Conor Woods. He was based in Chester in England, more flights and costs. He told me that there was a possibility that a Mr Braithwaite may be able to operate on me. I walked into his surgery in discomfort, limping slightly, with a pair of trainers and the one and a half-inch heel inserts that had been recommended. It was now coming up to a year since the accident. He shook his head as I walked into his practice room. I was asked to walk across the room several times in bare feet then he started to examine me. After a minute or two, he honed in on the area of my Achilles tendon. He pressed firmly in the spot where I now knew my Achilles had ruptured and I nearly hit the roof. It was as if he had pushed a needle into the area and delivered an electric shock. He apologised, 'I'm sorry, you don't like that spot do you?'
'No doctor.'

I didn't elaborate. I was now at the stage of not wanting to tell members of the medical profession what was wrong with me and where the problem was because they always told me they knew best. *Doctor is always right.* Yet Mr Braithwaite was different, I guessed that he knew exactly where the problem was. He asked me what medication I was on.

'Co-codomol pain relief.'

There were tears of sympathy in his eyes, 'Oh these are terrible, horrendous on the stomach.'

I thought to myself -Tell me something I don't know.

We exchanged pleasantries while he conducted a thorough examination on me, I was there almost an hour and eventually, I posed the question. 'So, will you be able to operate on me?'

He looked confused, 'You are here for a medical-legal report, nothing more. You have an inoperable condition Mrs Taylor, you are functionally disabled.'

'Conor Woods said you could possibly operate on me.'

'I'm afraid not. You need adaptions to your home, help with everything, any work you undertake will be severely affected and I hope my report goes some way in getting you the assistance you clearly need.'

On the way home from the airport with Kevin, I was

sobbing uncontrollably and was very distressed that he couldn't operate on me. Kevin had to hold me as I nearly fainted. Everyone was staring so I had to pull myself together.

His report didn't hold back. I received the same copy that Conor Woods did within 10 days. It was 21 pages long. It listed how my condition affected my day to day living, washing, dressing and such like. He said that I wasn't able to bear weight on my foot and in severe discomfort permanently despite steroids, acupuncture, physiotherapy and numerous visits to specialists. He said that I had an 'equinus deformity'. He mentioned lower back and leg pain and sciatica concluding that he did not envisage me getting back to running or regular gym work. He noted that I was in a 'static state' with ongoing significant symptoms and functional deficit attributable to the accident. He said that my left ankle deformity was permanent.

18

Lies and Tears

It was the political theorist Thomas Paine who wrote in his book, The Age of Reason (1795), 'One step above the sublime makes the ridiculous; and one step above the ridiculous, makes the sublime again.'

In another world, it could have been a perfect chapter heading to my medical review with Gary Colleary. It was coming up to two years since my accident. From the moment I stepped into his surgery, it was almost farcical. I had had a particularly bad day, as I'd taken a short walk around the estate. I'd probably pushed myself a little too far and fought the urge to pop yet another painkiller. I was only there for a review, after which he would write to my doctor who in turn would send another letter to DLA in the hope that they would review my level of disability.

As I walked into the room, with his full studious gaze upon me, I felt like a three-legged cart-horse bound for the knacker's yard. He spoke. A huge smile plastered across his face, 'Oh Diane, you are so much better today, those steroids must have helped enormously.'

I looked at Kevin and then back to the doctor waiting for him to deliver the punch line.

'You have to be kidding me,' I said.

'Not at all, your whole movement is better, the way you walk, you look so much more at ease.'

I glanced over at Kevin. Our eyes met and telepathically we delivered the same message -What is he on?

He proceeded to examine me and commented that the swelling to my ankle was down. I couldn't argue with that. He was right. That was the one thing that Kevin had said the steroids had achieved. I replied, 'That may be the case doctor, but my movement is no better.'

During the examination, we held a conversation that quickly escalated into an argument and once again he more or less accused me of faking the injury. I got more and more agitated, to the point where I was on the verge of tears. He told me to put my sock and shoe back on.

'I don't know what's wrong with you Diane. You know there are worse people than you.'

'I understand doctor, there must be a million people in worse condition than I am but all I ask is that somebody treats me, or operates on me, just so that I can walk normally again. Surely that's not too much to ask?'

I told him about Mr Braithwaite's report, 'He said I was inoperable with high amounts of pain, He said I was functionally disabled.'

He was shaking his head.

'If you don't believe me, I can send you a copy of the report.'

He was raising his voice, 'Unbelievable, unbelievable.'

I was losing my temper, 'Are you calling me a liar doctor, do you think I want to hobble around like an old crippled lady?'

He stood up and started waving his arms around, he looked over at Kevin, 'That's it, I can't work with this lady.'

'That's fine.'

'And I don't want to see you again.'

I am ashamed to admit it, but I reached for my coat and stomped out of the room. Kevin stayed behind and tried to reason with him but he wouldn't have it.

Once I got into the car I broke down into tears. What had I ever done to Gary Colleary? Two appointments from hell, as if I were the arch-enemy. It was even more frustrating because at this time he was in possession of Ingrid's report detailing her physiotherapy treatment, my lack of mobility and my chronic regional pain syndrome. 'Never mind,' Kevin said. 'You don't have to go back. He'll get the letter off to Dr Crothers and then she'll write to the DLA. If we get your DLA increased it would have been worth the aggravation.'

He did indeed write a letter to Dr Crothers although at that time I didn't know the content of his report. Gary Colleary wrote that, 'She (Diane) is much better,' he never mentioned the chronic regional pain syndrome, or my continued lack of mobility and told Dr Crothers that I could flex my foot to neutral. He put at the bottom of the letter that I had been aggressive towards him.

Dr Crothers followed up Gary Colleary's letter with her letter to the DLA. For some reason, which I will never fully understand, she mentioned my previous condition of bulimia, and the period in the past where I had self-harmed. Instead of focusing on my high disability and chronic pain, she chose to focus on stuff from 25 years ago which wasn't relevant to my disability. She had stated that I had 'restricted insight' but 18 months previously she had stated I had 'a walking disability, chronic pain and full insight'. The DLA was quick to respond. They told me that they had withdrawn all benefits, and now I did not qualify for even the lowest payment.

Two years after my accident, I finally met with someone who appeared to be taking my condition seriously. Bill Bird is a Canadian who moved to England as a youngster and has his workshop in Gloucestershire. Desmond Kennedy, a footwear expert from Cork recommended him, and I recall him saying to me, 'If you are a fake don't bother going, because he will find you out.' This was a deep-rooted concern of mine. I knew there were people within the medical profession and one or two other individuals, who believed I was faking my injury. What a ludicrous and hurtful suggestion. Why would I want to do that? The days had turned to weeks, the weeks had turned to months and the months had now turned into years. My life had drastically changed out of all recognition, I was almost housebound and every outdoor pursuit I had enjoyed so much prior to the accident had been stripped away from me.

I found Bill on the Internet. I read that he had a foot deformity himself, which is why he became interested in how bespoke shoes were made. He had worked in London's West End with some of the finest shoe craftsmen in England. After such a long time, I had more or less resigned myself to the fact that I would never walk correctly again. I told Kevin that a visit to him wouldn't do any harm. OK, I accepted that there were certain things that I would never be able to do again, running for example, but perhaps someone like Bill would understand what was happening to my foot and my body. If anyone could make me some footwear that would at least improve my whole posture, then it would be worthwhile. I read with interest that Bill worked with war veterans, men and women, who had been injured in explosions during conflict. We flew into the UK. More expense that we could do without but Sophia covered all the expenses.

I walked into his workshop and he immediately told me to remove my shoes. He studied the insoles and the heel inserts. 'Who fitted these?' He asked with a look of concern on his face.

'The National Health Service in Belfast,' I replied.

He said, 'They are a disgrace.' He pointed to a bin in the corner and said, 'They belong in there.'

Bill had sensors on the floor of his workshop. He explained that the sensors would measure my gait. I sighed. A Gait Machine, something that had been mentioned so long ago and yet was never actioned. He explained that the sensors were linked to a computer, as I walked they would produce a pattern on the computer which would be analysed. As I started to walk up and down his workshop, Bill sat at a computer screen and studied it intently. I glanced over and I noticed a series of squiggly lines starting to form on the screen. 'Keep walking,' Bill called over several times. Then he shook his head, 'Keep walking.'

I was with Bill for over four hours. It was the first time since my injury that I could recall an individual taking time over me. My experience in the past was that the medical professionals I had come into contact with couldn't wait to see the back of me. That may sound harsh, but I even felt that my physiotherapy appointments at times were rushed, the clock was ticking; the next patient was already waiting. Bill concluded the session by sitting me down and telling me that I had a serious deformity.

He repeated that the insoles were a disgrace. 'Woefully inadequate,' he said, 'and you are subconsciously throwing 78% of your body weight onto your good foot. As a result, your whole body has been affected, your knees, hips and back are in a real mess and the muscle wastage on your left leg is around 10%.'

I thought quietly to myself - So I'm not faking it.

Bill Bird fitted me with 85 mm insoles and heels, told me I would need specially made shoes for the rest of my life and warned that, because they would need to be specially made, they would not be cheap.

It was a great relief to me when, after just a few days walking with Bill's specially made insoles, I started to walk a bit better, my hip and back settled down and there was no uneven yanking movement as I walked. Although the walking improved a little, I felt like I was walking around on stilts. I cried tears of relief and joy, but also tears of frustration that for two years nobody in NHS Northern Ireland had had the foresight to put me on a Gait Machine and subsequently recommend someone like Bill Bird. Sophia paid for his report.

Bill Bird was very scathing of the Orthotics Department of Musgrave Hospital and the orthotics they fitted me with. He said that I had a clear 9 mm leg length discrepancy and because I had walked for 18 months in inadequate shoes, my condition had become worse. I had to smile when I read, 'It is very unusual for an ankle sprain to cause a 9 mm leg length discrepancy.'

Bill Bird's costings nearly gave me heart failure! I wondered how on earth anybody afforded that sort of price for shoes, although I did understand they were hand made. He went into specific details as to why I needed made to measure ankle boots and knee boots in a thoroughly comprehensive and detailed report. He provided photographs and charts of the Gait Machine print outs and concluded with my footwear requirements and costs. The top line read '2 pairs of dress shoes at £1,330 per pair.' The ankle and knee-length boots, sandals, trainers and beachwear sandals came to just over £10,000. I nearly fainted, though he did tell me that they should last four years. I showed the costings to Kevin. There was no way we could we afford to go ahead with Bill Bird's recommendations. We made an appointment with Conor Woods and I sent him Bill's report. It was now more important than ever for our solicitors to bring the issue of compensation to a conclusion. I mentioned an interim payment from the insurance company. I'd read that it was a usual procedure.

Conor Woods made a note in his legal pad and said he would put it to their solicitors.

In years two and three, I made the best of a bad situation. Thanks to Bill Bird, my ability to walk short distances unaided improved with his insoles and inserts. However, I was still unable to work or gain any semblance of independence and going out of the house on my own was still a step too far. Even sitting in the same position for longer than around 30 minutes was a challenge. My whole body appeared to rebel and so even a simple office job was out of the question. There was no interim payment forthcoming and therefore I couldn't afford the shoes and boots that Bill Bird had recommended. By now, we owed Sophia over £19,000. I spent many a restless night worrying about money and I daresay Kevin did too.

Connor Woods said he had arranged for a visit to a pain expert, Dr Cooper. The insurance company had asked for a report to assess whether or not I was suffering from chronic pain. The reason he sent me to Dr Cooper was because of Mr Braithwaite's report stating I was in 'large amounts of pain, functionally disabled and had secondary issues with my knees and hips'. He also stated I needed adaptions to my home and a little help with shopping and housework.

I liked Dr Cooper from the beginning, just a nice guy who appeared genuinely concerned at the condition I was in. I spent some time with him and his words were very powerful. At times they frightened me and he was very scathing towards the medical professionals who I'd seen previously. 'I know nothing about you because your solicitors haven't even sent me any paperwork on your condition,' he said, 'but it's clear you haven't been managed correctly.' He spent a lot of time manipulating and twisting my ankle. He raised his eyebrows a lot, shook his head occasionally and made me walk across the room many times. 'Aren't you getting any other treatment apart from physio?'

'No.'

'They are going to leave you in this state?'

Now I was beginning to get worried. After a thorough examination which lasted nearly an hour, Dr Cooper took copious amounts of notes. He was scathing about my legal team. He said, 'You make sure you get on the phone to them and get your notes sent straight to me.' He wished me goodbye and said, 'I'll write up a pain report straight away.'

Kevin came back to collect me. He was waiting for me outside as I hobbled over to the car.

'How did that go?' he asked.

'OK, he was nice.'

'He's going to write a report?'

'Yes.'

'So, no problems?'

'No,' I said, 'other than he seemed quite worried about the condition they've left me in.'

'I'm not surprised,' Kevin said. 'Everybody knows how bad you are, apart from the Belfast Health Trust who continually deny there's anything wrong with you.' As Kevin pushed the car into gear and drove away he said, 'The same trust Dr Cooper works for.'

I turned to face him, 'What do you mean?'

'Nothing,' he shook his head, 'I'm probably just being paranoid but, to me, that's a conflict of interest.

'What are you saying?'

'I'm just saying I hope he is honest that's all.'

I told Kevin he was too suspicious. I had no doubt that Dr Cooper was a genuine man. I smiled as I told Kevin that Dr Cooper personally assured me that his report would be written up immediately. After two weeks I hadn't heard back from the solicitors so I called them. I was passed around a bit and then a secretary confirmed that they hadn't received the report. I was a little disappointed as Dr Cooper had clearly stated it would be prepared straight away.

The following month I was told the delay was

because Dr Cooper was on sick leave. I asked Conor Woods once again about an interim payment. 'I'm working on it,' he told me.

'It would help if I were able to get those shoes from Bill Bird.'

'I'll chase it up.'

I called every week and after two months I was tearing my hair out. Things were at a standstill. I was still in the same condition physically and getting more depressed by the day. As well as Dr Cooper's report, I was also waiting for a carers report to be obtained. The report should have detailed all of the normal daily living tasks I was unable to do. After three months had passed, I rang Conor Wood's office and found myself speaking to him directly. 'Has Dr Cooper's report arrived?' I asked.

'No.'

I was on the verge of tears. He could hear that I was upset as my voice began to break. 'Has his office given any sort of explanation or any indication when it   will   be   coming?'

'No, I can't explain why at the moment, we are as mystified as you Diane.'

I got a call from Conor Wood the night before the care person was due out to my home. He told me that he hadn't received Dr Cooper's report because he wouldn't be writing one. There was no explanation. He also said that the care person had cancelled for the following day as she would be working off the chronic pain report which was not yet written. I was distressed and crying. I had waited for months and months on these reports. 'We have some good news. We have a meeting with the insurance company. They are prepared to talk about a settlement.'

He threw me into confusion, 'But the carers report hasn't been submitted. How can they talk about a settlement for the chronic pain?'

He was direct and to the point, 'They are not prepared to settle on the chronic pain issue, they don't accept you have chronic pain.'

'Well no, Mr Woods, they won't, because two reports which would categorically point to the fact I have chronic pain, haven't arrived so they won't have seen them.'

Mr Woods still wanted the meeting to go ahead, but the difference in the claim would make a huge difference in the settlement.

'No,' I said. 'Absolutely not.'

I'm ashamed to say I ended the call abruptly.

19

Consulting the Specialists

Two days later I took another phone call from McIvor Farrell. It appeared I had won a small victory with Conor Woods because he notified me that he had arranged for a consultation with a chronic pain specialist, Dr Kirkor. The only slight problem was that he was in the UK, in Birmingham. 'And how much will that cost me?' I said.

'£900.'

'How much?'

'They don't come cheap these blokes Diane, I'm sure

it will be worth it.'

'OK, that's progress,' I said, 'but why can't we get anyone to do it in Northern Ireland?'

'We just can't,' he said. 'We just can't.'

I was getting a bad feeling about this and when I told Kevin after I ended the call, he looked at me as if to say - I told you so. It was Kevin who first suggested that getting a balanced and fair report from Dr Cooper might be problematic because of a conflict of interests. Were the relevant specialists in the Belfast area closing ranks? Was Dr Cooper persuaded against writing the report because he wanted to tell the truth about my real condition?

I travelled to Birmingham with Sophia, we flew from Belfast International Airport and she tried to cheer me up by telling me it was a few days of *girlie fun*. I couldn't drum up the same enthusiasm as her especially because I had to go into a wheelchair and be pushed around both airports. I can fully understand the elderly fighting the decision that they eventually have to admit they can't walk and a wheelchair is the only practical way to get around. Whichever way you look at it, it's demeaning, almost like you are holding your hands up and admitting defeat. I felt everyone was looking at me, pointing the finger. Sophia tried to make light of it as she pushed me along cheerfully but I just kept my head down and prayed we wouldn't bump into anyone we knew.

We booked into a nice hotel for the night. On day two we had our appointment. I had come prepared with a photograph of the stair lift we had installed in the house, a report that also confirmed damage to my hips, the details of my treatments and the night splint which I was now wearing every night. It had been given to me by a physiotherapist in Musgrave. I also had a report on my restricted ability and the medication I was taking for the pain. I had it all in a cardboard folder.

I explained to Dr Kirkor the situation with Dr Cooper, how he had promised a true and honest report that had somehow disappeared from the radar and that, mysteriously, my solicitor couldn't find me a specialist pain consultant in Northern Ireland. As I slid the folder across his desk, I said, 'All I want is a true, honest account doctor. From day one, I feel I have been neglected and let down.'

He didn't even look up from his notes. He slid the folder back across the desk to me. 'I don't need to see these; I'll do a good report.'

I was puzzled, 'But my solicitor said I should bring evidence of my pain and disability.'

'I have all the evidence I need.'

I looked over at Sophia. She just shrugged her shoulders.

He asked me to take off my shoe and sock, moved around the desk and signalled for me to lift my leg. He took my ankle in his right hand while he held my calf with his left. I gritted my teeth, this was going to hurt. From experience with the medical specialists and doctors, this signalled a prolonged assault on my ankle, several minutes of twisting and manipulation. Dr Kirkor eased my ankle back and forward gently, no more than an inch in each direction. A little pain but worse was to come, I was sure. He took his finger gently over the area of the damaged tendon. It almost felt like a pleasant massage. 'OK,' he said, 'you can put your shoe back on.'

'That's it?' I joked.'

'Yes.'

'What! Don't you want me to walk across the room to see the extent of my disability?'

'No, I saw you when you walked it.'

'Yes, with shoes with orthopaedic heels, in bare feet I can't even put my heel on the floor.'

He held up his hand, it was a signal to stop.

'I've seen enough, you can go now.'

I was flabbergasted and struggled for words. I

looked at my watch; we had been in there 10 minutes. I thought of the cost, the hotel, and the general expenses. It had cost just short of a thousand pounds plus the £900 consultancy fee and once again Sophia had paid because of the struggle I had to make ends meet. I felt genuinely cheated and worked it out quickly. Nine hundred pounds for ten minutes, that's an hourly rate of over £5,000, but more important than that, how could he write a fair and honest report given such a quick appointment?

I think he sensed my concern. 'Don't worry Mrs Taylor, I have enough information to write up a good report.' What did that mean exactly? Had he seen enough to realise the pain I was in? Was he on my side? Was his report exactly what my solicitor required?

I was worried about receiving Dr Kirkor's report. In a nutshell, I hadn't been in his surgery long enough for him to have made an accurate assessment. I voiced my concerns to Sophia on the flight back but she told me not to worry. 'Look at it the other way Mum,' she said. 'He's a good doctor, he didn't need to examine you for two hours to see the pain and discomfort you were in.'

I sat back in the seat, enjoying the cup of airline tea I had just been served. I told myself - She's right. If only Dr Kirkor had seen me at the airport. I had declined a wheelchair at first as my ankle was having one of its better days. However, after a walk in the cold across the airport car park, I needed a wheelchair to get me to the departure gate, my hips and sciatic nerve deciding to throw a spanner in the works. 'He is working for you Mum,' Sophia continued. 'Your solicitor recommended him.' Yet something was bothering me. It was a 10 minute *getting to know you* meeting, not a medical consultation in any shape or form.

I was stunned when I read Dr Kirkor's report. He had reviewed the reports from the hospital, other GPs diagnoses as well as expert testimonies from Mr Braithwaite, Mr Andrews and Bill Bird and had copied line for line their observations and comments. It was more than six pages of simply copying and pasting sentences and paragraphs from other people. It made Dr Kirkor's report look fairly comprehensive at face value. But it was when I read the last page and a half, where he gave his *impression and opinion*, that the full horror of what he was saying became apparent.

I don't know who this doctor was working for but it certainly wasn't me, and a good conspiracy theorist wouldn't have taken too long to suggest that he appeared to be working for the other side, the solicitors and insurance company of the contractor we were pursuing through the courts. It was a tissue of lies. He said I walked normally in shoes and that my ankle was not painful when he pushed against it with his hands. To be honest, that was probably the only truth he told in his report because he had hardly flexed my ankle at all. He said there was no visible swelling and the pulse on each ankle was the same, 'regular and normal'. By all accounts my back was fine too, 'lumber spine unrestricted and the claimant presents no sign of chronic regional pain syndrome'.

My hands were shaking, I struggled to breathe. This was my worst nightmare. I thought of the ridiculous expense flying over to see him. But worse was to come. 'In my opinion, on the balance of probabilities, there is a substantial emotional/psychological element of the claimant's symptoms.' He said the fact that I had a stair lift fitted at home and had a disabled badge was 'not entirely reasonable'. There it was in black and white, a so-called pain expert had called me a liar and despite numerous medical reports detailing ankle, leg, back and hip-related injuries and immobility, he had said it was all in my head. I'd had four years of Hell. It was the lowest point I had ever been in my life.

I was called to a meeting with Conor Woods, in the

halls of the High Court; he had brought the barrister with him. We wondered what it was all about, was there a settlement to be discussed? I took Kevin and Sophia with me, we all sensed it would be a defining moment.

What happened next was rather strange. We could see Conor Woods standing with someone who we assumed was the barrister, an elderly man with grey hair. Conor Woods looked over and noticed us. I expected him to acknowledge the fact we were there but he didn't, he turned his back on us and continued with his conversation. I didn't want to be rude and despite Kevin saying we should go over, I said, 'No.' He'd seen us. He'd make contact when he was ready. We took a seat in the hall of the court.

Conor Woods made us wait 20 minutes. All the while he stood with his back to us.

Eventually, he wandered over. 'I'm sorry, I didn't see you.' What rubbish, we were the only people there. I decided not to say anything. I was right, he wanted to talk settlement figures. I dared to wonder if this was as a result of Mr Braithwaite's report and the report from Bill Bird. At least a reasonable settlement would mean closure, allow me to make changes to the house, perhaps afford some help at home to do the things I couldn't manage and take a little pressure from Kevin and Sophia. The elderly barrister barely introduced himself before he got down to business. He said, 'This is a case of a twisted ankle.'

I said, 'Excuse me, have you read Mr Braithwaite's report and the hip report, and all the other reports?'

He said, 'What hip report?'

'And Bill Bird's report?'

'He's just a shoe salesman,' the barrister interrupted. 'It will count for nothing in court.'

I was flabbergasted, 'Just a shoe salesman? He has treated over 4000 war veterans. He's the most respected consultant in his field.'

'A shoe salesman nonetheless.'

'My daughter paid more than £2000 for that report, I was with him for four hours and he put me on a Gait Machine linked to a computer.'

'Kirkor's report said …'

I cut him short, 'I was in Kirkor's surgery for 10 minutes, are you telling me that's the report you are focusing on?'

He looked at Woods as if to say help me out.

I continued, 'The computer analysed my walking style, it printed out a graph like a lie detector test, said my whole body was out of kilter as a result of my injury.'

He pounced, 'Oh, I know all about you and your lie detector tests,' he raised his hand towards the ceiling.

'There's a file on you this high.'

Sophia was flabbergasted.

I turned to Woods, 'Tell me this isn't happening, is he working for me or the insurance company?'

Perhaps in hindsight, I shouldn't have said that but it was exactly how it appeared. Their familiarity was at times alarming. The barrister's job was to go into court to get me the best settlement possible. He had been supplied with an armoury of information, testimonies and reports from medical professionals and experts in their respective fields. Reports that had cost thousands of pounds and yet he was holding onto, as far as I'm concerned, a fake report. It was, in my opinion, written by a fraudster conducting a sham examination. We couldn't quite believe what was taking place.

Kevin could hold his tongue no longer, 'Aren't you supposed to be on our side? What about the night splint that she wears every night to keep her foot at a right angle so she doesn't wake up in agony in the morning.'

He said, 'Sure I wear one of them myself.'

Kevin said, 'Are you joking?'

He turned to me, 'Take your shoe off Diane. Show him how you walk.'

I looked at poor Sophia who was in tears.

'A twisted ankle,' Kevin said. 'You actually believe that a twisted ankle could do this sort of damage.'

I looked at the barrister. 'Tell me honestly, do you think I have imagined this? Do you think this pain is in my head?'

'Yes,' he said categorically.

I looked at Woods. 'And you?'

He didn't have time to answer because the barrister was walking away. He had packed his papers into his briefcase and was strutting off along the corridor waving his hands at Woods in a gesture that said it was over and he didn't want the case. Conor Woods looked at him as he almost ran out of the building and eventually disappeared.

I turned to Woods. 'This whole thing stinks. It's nothing more than corruption because whoever he is working for, it certainly isn't me.'

Woods looked lost.

'What happens now?' Kevin asked.

Woods shrugged his shoulders and walked away.

Seven days later I received a letter from McIvor Farrell. It said that after nearly five years of representation they regretted that because of my refusal to accept there was a psychological element to my chronic pain, they had taken the decision that they were unable to act on my behalf.

I spent several nights replaying over in my mind the consultation with Dr Kirkor. I came to the conclusion that before he even met me, he had made his mind up about exactly what he was going to write in his report. He had been briefed beforehand, as had the barrister. They had both been approached, their minds influenced. That was the only explanation.

20

A New Legal Team

So we started all over again after my solicitors of five years dropped me like a stone because I refused to acknowledge that the pain was in my head. The word traumatic doesn't even come near it. I thought back to the day Conor Woods called and told me we had a meeting with the barrister. I was full of optimism, dared to dream that a little closure was in the air by way of a financial settlement that would allow me to pay back the money I owed to my daughter and move on. That's all I wanted to do, move on. I had accepted my disability and even learned how to cope with the pain … most days.

A close friend, Alex Eason from the Democratic Unionist Party (DUP) referred me to a firm of solicitors, Hunts, and I went to meet Paddy Hunt, who was going to act for me. He told me categorically, that McIvor Farrell and Conor Woods had not been honest about my injury. He quoted big figures to me, or rather bigger figures than the barrister of Conor Woods had promised and initially, I felt confident with Paddy. He seemed quite nice, professional and optimistic about where we were heading. Paddy said, 'I have your back. Somebody needs to have your back. I am not going to stop until you get every penny you're meant to get.' Paddy had my back alright, to stab me in it. He was nothing more than a wolf in sheep's clothing. He was worse than the first set of solicitors because he promised me everything, but delivered nothing.

I requested my files from Conor Woods. They took three months to return them to me, three months before Paddy could even take a brief look at them. I called McIvor Farrell's offices most weeks and was fed a tissue of lies as to why they couldn't release the files. In the meantime, Paddy Hunt and his team had costed out what he termed was a reasonable claim. It detailed all aspects of disability, home improvements, loss of earnings, Bill Bird's shoes over a lifetime and the pain and distress caused since the accident. It came to over a million pounds.

Eventually, I got the files from McIvor Farrell and was able to give them to my new legal team. They appointed two new barristers. They wanted to send me back to Mr Andrews for an update because he had clearly stated in his report that he suspected chronic regional pain syndrome. Kevin also suggested a new care report, because my condition had worsened. I should have noticed the warning signs there and then. One of the barristers, Mel Powers, was vehemently opposed to any new care report, 'Let's not even go there,' he said.
'Why not?' Kevin asked. 'She is in a worse condition. Surely it makes sense?'

Eventually, we all agreed to wait for Mr Andrew's new report, to see what it said. We made an appointment and I attended the meeting some weeks later. His new report was puzzling, to say the least. He wrote that I complained about chronic regional pain syndrome but failed to elaborate on the Achilles damage or the scarring that had been previously discussed with Kevin. All in all, the report fell someway short in the content department. If I were to take a guess I would suggest it was a bit rushed.

On several occasions, I spoke with Fionnuala Hunt suggesting to her that Mr Andrews may wish to comment on the scar tissue on my Achilles and on the care I might need in the future as well as likely adaptations to my home. Either she didn't follow up my request or Mr Andrews never bothered. Mr Andrews was obviously protecting his bosses in the Belfast Health Trust, in my opinion. My legal team did action another care report and presented it to the defendants (at our expense). Janice Reid carried out a full assessment at my home when I was present and arrived at the conclusion that I would require 50 minutes of care each day for the rest of my life. This was costed in compensation terms at £250,000 alone.

I suggested to Fionnuala, that perhaps we needed to find 'a really good professional' to ascertain the pain levels I was suffering. She looked shocked and reminded me of Dr Kirkor and his sham report. 'Is that such a good idea?' she said. I was concerned that the insurance company's barristers would make a big play on Dr Kirkor's report and bring out his suggestion that the pain was in my head.

After this meeting with my legal team, I knew I had to obtain more evidence from outside the Belfast

Health Trust because no one was forthcoming with the truth about my ruptured Achilles tendon or the chronic state I'd been left in. My daughter's boyfriend, Stephen, had told me there was a top chiropodist in Bangor called Jim Patterson who had many years of experience in foot and ankle problems. If anyone would tell me the truth about my ruptured Achilles, it would be Jim.

The first time I met him, he took one look at the back of my Achilles and felt the scar tissue. He kept repeating, 'Oh my God! Oh my God! You have lots of scar tissue and your Achilles has definitely been ruptured.' He went on to show me a diagram of the foot, ankle and Achilles area and explained what happens when the Achilles ruptures. I thought to myself – What a relief, someone finally telling the truth. I asked Jim to write a report stating this information. He didn't disappoint and his report was given to my legal team, Hunt Solicitors.

Around this time, I also went to Dr Williams in Greenisland Health Centre who felt the scar tissue up and down my Achilles in front of Kevin. She said, 'Oh my goodness, there's a lot of scar tissue there and with you being stuck up on a 3.5 inch wedge for 12 hours a day, you must have arthritis in your knees and hips. She said she was going to send me for an x-ray. The x-ray confirmed this one month later but, before she could give me the results, she was moved on to another health centre. Those results were given to Fionnnuala Hunt and she passed them onto Mr Andrews. She made an appointment for this to be updated on my medical notes with Mr Andrews but that appointment was cancelled. Why? My care report should have been updated because I now had more evidence to prove that I had been seriously injured.

The insurance company was being fed information and were concerned about the carer's report we had actioned, detailing necessary care at 50 minutes a day and that I also needed a stair lift to ascend and descend my stairs safely. I was informed that they would be sending *their people* out to assess me. A middle-aged lady, Shirley Baird, turned up 30 minutes early for the appointment and because I was not ready, Kevin asked her to come back at the correct time. She was sitting in her car and I went and got her. I brought her into the house and apologised. As soon as she sat down, I thought I felt a connection with her as she said she had arthritis too and knew how I felt. What a nice lady I thought. How wrong I was. She was there a while. Her report was quite detailed. She stated:

* No need for need a stair lift.
* No help needed for cooking.
* No help needed shopping.
* No sign of pain showing.
And worst of all, it recommended no more help than;
* One Spring Clean per year.

As I read the report it all became clear. The legal process was farcical, a joke. It was as clear as day that the insurance company had given Shirley Baird her remit before she had even turned up at the house. It wouldn't have surprised me if her report had been prepared before she ever met me. How could two *professional carer* reports be so drastically different? Did this lady sincerely believe I would allow my daughter to pay for a stair lift I didn't need one? I explained to Shirley Baird, the circumstances surrounding the stair lift, that I couldn't afford one until my daughter stepped in and insisted she paid for it. When I showed Sophia the report and pointed out what Shirley Baird had said about the stair lift, she shook her head in dismay. She reminded me of how much I had fought against the idea of a stair lift, how she insisted that I had one installed as I crawled up the stairs to bed most nights of the week.

Fourteen months later, we were in court. Just a few days before court, the insurance company had the audacity to conspire against me and send my legal team, Fionnuala Hunt, an email stating they had information of a Diane Taylor doing a park fun run in a running club in Carrickfergus. Furthermore they sent a photo of this person, a silhouette of head and shoulders. You couldn't even make the person out. In my opinion, this was the tactic of an insurance company to mislead and cause me upset with lies and skulduggery. Over the weekend I investigated this Diane Taylor. She was a blonde female who looked nothing like me, which the insurance company would have been fully aware of.

The insurance company acting for the contractor had made an offer before we even got there. They wanted to save court costs and barrister fees and had lodged an offer much lower than the million pounds the claim had been valued at. During my initial discussion with my barrister, he advised us to accept £100,000. I couldn't quite believe it. Kevin and Sophia were both with me for support and I could see the disappointment on their faces. We knew it was a game between the barristers and suspected they would battle it out in the corridors of the courts. I was more than realistic that we wouldn't be seeing a settlement of a million pounds, but in all honesty, surely the settlement would be over £500,000?

The insurance company, by lodging a six-figure offer were admitting liability, that wasn't in dispute. It was now up to the barrister to get me the highest offer possible. The junior barrister chipped in, he started to talk about Shirley Baird's report and how it wouldn't look good in court. I said it was a sham and reminded him of the first carer's report, the one we had paid for. It said I needed 50 minutes of care each day for the rest of my life. I turned to the senior barrister, 'Shirley Baird's report is fake. You need to tell the court that. We need to bring Bill Bird in as a witness also Ingrid the physiotherapist and Janice Reid who said I needed a lifetime of care.'

There then followed an uncomfortable silence.

Then it dawned on me, 'They're not here are they?'

He shook his head.

'But why? I instructed you to bring them here as witnesses for me.'

At that point, Shirley Baird walked past us. She dipped her head as she passed, didn't make eye contact.

'But she's here,' I pointed.

'You need to accept their offer,' he repeated.

My world was falling apart at the seams. The biggest day of my life, a day that would affect my entire future was slowly unravelling because my legal team couldn't even manage to get my witnesses into court.

'What's happened?' I asked. 'Why isn't Bill or Janice here? Why aren't my witnesses here?'

He didn't answer.

'You haven't called them, have you?'

He shook his head slightly then stated, 'It's a decent offer, you need to take it. You don't even have to go through with this.'

'But I want to go through with it, I've nothing to hide. I've been living with this for seven bloody years!'

I referred to the reports about my hip, Jim Patterson's report and the physiotherapist's report. I turned to the junior barrister who was supposed to be in my corner. He shrugged his shoulders.

'You haven't read them?' I questioned in horror.

'No, I haven't seen them.'

I started to well up and tremble with rage as the full impact of what he had just said, hit me. My barrister, the man who was supposed to represent me in court hadn't read any of the reports that confirmed everything I'd said for years instead, he preferred to quote from a report that had been actioned by the other side. He said if I wanted to go into court, I would be the first witness on the stand. I sincerely believe he said that to try and frighten me, to put me off.

Sophia was getting upset, telling the barristers that I

would make a horrible witness because I was angry and agitated. They would have a field day with me she said. She knew me too well! They were ill-prepared and because I insisted that we go into court they threw me to the wolves. I was an hour and a half on the stand. Their sole remit was to wind me up and make me lose my temper. They referred to all the reports that painted me in a negative light and simply didn't mention any of the reports that found in my favour. Bill Bird's computer analysis from the Gait Machine which proved that 78% of my bodyweight subconsciously leaned away from my damaged ankle was never addressed.

After they had finished with me, they asked Sophia to take the stand. Sophia was a good witness. She tried to explain what help and care I needed and how seriously injured I was, that she was pushing me about in wheelchairs and I was using mobility scooters on holiday. They didn't want to know. They got her off the stand as quickly as possible. She was up there for no more than 15 minutes.

Daniel Prokop once wrote, 'Even amidst tragedy there is laughter, sometimes farce. The degree of farce depends on who is running the tragedy.' This summed it up perfectly for me, that scandalous first day in court where I didn't know whether to laugh or cry and the degree of farce depended on who was running it. Their barrister had a field day, I think he enjoyed every minute and yet at times, I sensed he even felt a bit sorry for me because it was David against Goliath, and my barristers had taken away my stones and my slingshot.

I spoke from the heart with passion and conviction but, dare I say, not belief because I knew that I had been shafted by the legal system, the game; the big, rigged game of law. On the second day, one of my barristers didn't show up! Was that because the day before he threatened me and my family members? He said that if I didn't take the amount lodged into court, I would be hit with an avalanche and a tonne of bricks. He had my daughter so distressed with his threats she didn't sleep that night.

My legal team advised me on the second day, that I wasn't getting a penny from my care report. They said both surgeons for both parties were going to sign a legal document to state I didn't need any help, any adaptions to my home or a stair lift. I said that the care report should have been given to Mr Andrews 14 months ago and that none of my witnesses were there either. I told them I was going to have to represent myself because it was a farce. They told me if I didn't trust them then they wouldn't represent me. 'Great,' I said. 'If you don't want to represent me, I will represent myself.'

'Fine.'

'Give me my files.'

'You can't have them.'

'How can I represent myself if I don't have my files?'

'Not our problem, we want paid before you can get your files.'

We were ushered towards the side rooms and given some coffee. When I was in there I met Jim Patterson, the chiropodist who had also examined me and was there as a witness if required. I had seen him a few months after I employed Hunt's legal team and he had written a report to say there was evidence of a ruptured Achilles tendon. I perked up a little when I saw Jim, I asked him if my team had called him as a witness. He shook his head sadly. 'I've seen them, Diane, offered to take the stand but it's clear they don't want me in there.'

'What? But why?'

'You make your own mind up, better still, ask them.'

'But ... '

'In my opinion, those barristers are the most bent, corrupt and dishonourable profession in the world.'

I was *in the zone* at this point. I was determined to represent myself as I had done years previously and I knew I would do a better job than them at getting to the truth. I was past caring about money at this point, I was determined to get the truth out in court about my ruptured Achilles, the scar tissue, chronic pain and care needs. I was eager to get Mr Andrews in the witness box to ask him questions about the ruptured Achilles tendon and I relayed this to my solicitor.

In the meantime, I didn't notice anything that was going on in the hall, I was so focused. About 30 or 40 minutes had passed and Kevin told me to look at Mr Andrews. 'He's biting his nails and look at Shirley Baird, she's a nervous wreck.' Was this because they were going to be cross-examined by me? And were worried about perjuring themselves in the stand?

They came up with another offer, it was 40% more than my legal team suggested I would get but I said I still wasn't happy. I wanted to represent myself; it was nowhere near enough to cover even my basic care needs. I said again, 'I want my files.' They threatened me, said I would wait more than six months for my files, which would have taken my lawsuit to over eight years. I owed my daughter tens of thousands of pounds and at this point. She was extremely upset and pleaded with me to settle. It wasn't about the money anymore; it was about my sanity and my daughter's sanity. In my head, I knew I was going to get my story out, one way or another. I was going to make damn sure they would never do this to another person. In the words of my childhood heroine, Scarlett O'Hara, 'I can't fight this today, I will fight it tomorrow, after all, tomorrow is another day.'

There was a final twist in the tale. Jim Patterson referred me to another specialist. He was private and expensive but I figured that if he could put me under the knife and make right whatever was wrong, then it would be worth the £20,000 or £30,000 it might cost me. At least the compensation might be of some use.

Mr Kilmartin was based in Hillsborough. A Podiatric Surgeon, he was elected the first Dean of the Faculty of Podiatric Surgery in 1998. He was a highly respected specialist and I dared to dream that perhaps he might be able to get to the bottom of my injury, even operate. Fingers crossed. He put an ultrasound on the Achilles tendon area. He examined me thoroughly and made me do a series of walks and stretches. I couldn't hold my tongue any longer, 'So doctor, can you operate?'

He pointed to a screen. I edged forward in my seat. 'This probably doesn't show you an awful lot but it tells me everything I need to know. This area here,' he said, 'is your ankle and your heel and this area is your Achilles tendon.' He pointed again, 'This dark area shouldn't be here.'

He explained a bit about the lines in the tissue, and that they should be running parallel like tree rings. He explained the dark area was the scarring on the Achilles tendon. At last … someone was telling the truth! He asked three questions, 'Have you been diagnosed with an Achilles rupture? Have you been diagnosed with scar tissue? Have you been diagnosed with chronic regional pain syndrome?'

I said, 'No, I haven't.'

'Well,' he said, 'you have all three.'

Mr Kilmartin said if he operated on my Achilles tendon, he would intensify the chronic pain so much so that, if I put my foot on the ground, I would not be able to walk and I would be in even more pain. He suggested another surgeon in England, who could possibly cut my calf to try and drop the heel, but it was halfway up my lower limb, with a success rate of only 50%. I'd sought out every medical professional under the sun for seven years and they'd tried to tell me it was in my head. I had a twisted ankle, no more. Even my legal team had said it was nothing more than a twisted ankle. At last, here was someone with integrity, just like Jim Patterson who had told the truth about my injury. It was a relief. The truth was out. It was over, their game was up. Mr Kilmartin was an honest man. He could have easily bled my bank account dry with false promises and bullshit but he didn't. It was inoperable. The chances of any success were very slim he said, and because of the age of the injury any surgery would likely worsen my condition.

His final words were that it wasn't worth the risk.

I sent the new evidence from Mr Kilmartin to Fionnuala Hunt and I asked her to go back to the insurance company and to make sure my care needs were met for life with this new evidence, which proved I was a lot more seriously injured than all the experts had made out. She dismissed this new evidence and said my case was finished with.

Kevin

It was May 2012, when my partner changed. It was nothing more than an innocuous accident on a pavement that a contractor really shouldn't have left in that condition. It was painful and, of course, worrying at the time. We all thought it was nothing, a minor injury, easily repaired and she would be back on her feet in no time, after all, we had the best National Health Service in the world.

Diane was a fun-loving, energetic girl, slim and extremely fit, the life and soul of any party, confident and outgoing. She enjoyed running, visiting the gym, walking the dogs, dancing and hillwalking, but most of all she enjoyed long shopping trips and holidays with our daughter Sophia. Me, I was more than happy to stay at home dog sitting. The pleasure I got watching the excitement on Diane's and Sophia's faces before any such trip made up for the fact I wouldn't be going. Any loving partner and father will tell you, seeing your loved one and daughter ecstatically happy is a price worth paying.

Diane loved to travel and in the years prior to that fateful day she had visited New York, Tenerife, Prague, Berlin, Paris, Barcelona, Greece and the UK and enjoyed a few Caribbean cruises. Life was good, we were quite affluent and the shellfish business I was in at the time seemed like a licence to print money. That all changed the day I helped to lift her into the casualty department of Antrim Area Hospital. A curtain was slowly lowered over the life she once knew, the life I once knew too. In many respects, that was the day I lost my partner but through no fault of her own.

Seven years on, our life bears no resemblance to the

life we once knew. The gym is a distant memory to Diane, as is hill walking, excursions to the beach with the dog or indeed walking of any description. A trip to the shops is now a major expedition. She can't go alone. Standing in a queue for more than a few minutes is impossible because of the discomfort and chronic pain. She is also stuck up on a 3.5 inch wedge for 12 hours a day for the rest of her life. I can't even fathom how she's going to cope in the years ahead.

Gone are the days when Diane would cook a romantic meal, or host a dinner party. She needs help just to wash the dishes; she needs help with daily shopping as queues are a *no no*. She sits on a stool to wash the dishes because she can't stand like anybody else and cooking anything more than beans on toast requires a herculean effort on her behalf. She's tried, believe me, she has, but it always ends in tears and frustration, a cry for help.

It's not just the pain, the discomfort and the immobility. Diane has changed and I'm convinced it's as a result of the seven years of disappointment, false promises, lack of honesty from health professionals and legal teams but, above all, the medication she has constantly been subjected to. She is a different character to the woman and mother I once knew and no wonder. She has, metaphorically speaking, gone 12 rounds with a heavyweight boxer and at the end of each of those 12 rounds she has been knocked to the canvas with force.

I started receiving phone calls at critical times. By critical times I mean critical for me and my shellfish business, collection and sales. So much depended on weather conditions, cyclical events, tides and of course the weekly exports. Of course, Diane didn't know any of the conditions and timings I was working to. Sometimes she just wanted a shoulder to lean on with a few kind and encouraging words; an ear to bend as she'd spent so long in the house on her own. Other times she felt well enough for a trip out but, of course, that meant usually being accompanied so I had to drop what I was doing to be her support, her crutch. Other times she had been really brave and confident and took it upon herself to take trips to the shops on her own. Sometimes she made it back home safe and sound and it was a phone call of exuberance at this simple achievement that others take for granted. Other times I'd get a phone call from a supermarket that Diane was immobile and distressed, her hip joint had given out or her sciatic nerve had seized up. More often than not she had simply overdone it and her ankle had cried 'no more!' I'd arrive to find her sitting in the corner of ASDA, distressed and embarrassed. It was the shame of it she always said, the shame of not being able to walk into a supermarket and choose a few things to make a meal for your loved ones.

I gave up the shellfish business which had been a team effort with me and Diane. She was not able to work on the shore or to help me run my business. She had been an integral part. I took on a job in construction, long hours with frequent, week-long stays in the UK. A part of me believed that because I was now working for someone, Diane would have to manage without me. If I were working somewhere like Newcastle, England, she wouldn't have any option. I couldn't come running. Sophia was at home but, then again, she was self-employed too and her business was growing. She was all over the north and the south of Ireland. Just like me, it was impossible for her to just drop everything and drive home. Diane was left to her own devices, she would have to cope.

Diane fought bravely. For a while, there were no phone calls at work and I dared to believe she had somehow turned a magical corner. After long stints of employment away, I returned to see a drastic change in my partner. She hadn't turned any corner instead she'd borne her illness bravely behind closed doors. The trips out to the supermarket and the gentle short walks around the estate had stopped completely. She'd resorted to painkillers and comfort eating and over the space of two and a half years she'd put on two stone. Her muscles, particularly on her legs, were wasting away. I handed my notice to my employer. My partner was more important to me than the income and, despite Diane's objections, I became her full-time carer, picking up casual part-time work whenever I could, as long as it was convenient to our lifestyle.

If there is a God, and I have my doubts, then surely he worked overtime to create our beautiful daughter Sophia. Not only did he bless her with looks and personality but he gave her kindness, compassion and generosity in abundance as well as unconditional love for her parents. She sat us down one day and told us not to worry about money. Her business was going from strength to strength and, although it would have been nice to invest for the future to develop and grow the business quickly, she said that her family always would come first. She put a pot of money into a bank account, said it was there for us and whatever Diane needed by way of mobility aids or private specialist treatment, she insisted on paying. I don't mind admitting that I shed a few quiet tears in bed that evening, tears of gratitude for the best daughter a father could ever hope to have, but also tears of sympathy and frustration for Diane. There were tears of frustration for myself because, as a father, I was unable to provide for my family, the one thing I had managed easily since the day Sophia was born.

We agreed on the financial assistance from Sophia. It lifted a huge weight from my mind because it gave me the flexibility to be there for Diane if and when she needed me but I insisted that Sophia create a loan account for us and we would repay it whenever we could. Incredibly, at one point, the debt rose as high as £30,000. Not once did our wonderful daughter put pressure on us to make any repayments.

I always knew how special our daughter was, from the moment she was born to the day she said her first words and when she took her first few steps. But the one good thing to have come from this *debacle*, and that's the perfect word to describe the mess of the last seven years, was to show Diane and me that our daughter truly was special … one in a million. To this day she continues with all aspects of her unwavering love, care and financial support.

Sophia

Before my mum's accident in May 2012, we had a very full and glamorous lifestyle. I have no siblings and so my mum and I are very close. We would holiday a few times a year and have lots of adventures together. My mum has several friends in the film industry and we would visit them every couple of weeks in Windsor and London for the weekend when school was finished.

We also visited different film sets as I had worked on some of these sets when I was finishing my GCSE's at school. The James Bond set at Leavesden Studios in England, Game of Thrones TV series and Clash of the Titans to name a few. We travelled to Tenerife and visited the Clash of the Titans movie set. I remember when we got up at 5 am and travelled up to Mount Tiede, the highest volcano on the island, to see the film set. The ground and set were uneven, all based on sand but we walked around for hours and met all the cast and crew. Mum was always up ahead, first everywhere and I was forever telling her to slow down.

My mum is a very stylish lady and would never be seen without her boots or her high heels.

We would always be out together, walking or jogging to Greenisland or Jordanstown several times a week. We would go to the gym and walk our two Labrador dogs together. Again Mum would always take the lead. I swear, if the dogs could have talked even they would have told her to slow down. She was a ball of energy. We would enjoy going out to Café Vaudeville at the weekends, my mum and I had always been known for our love of dancing. I now have a contract with this venue for my performers and the staff and management always ask about my mum and share memories of us coming in and dancing at the weekends – the memory of that makes me very sad.

We enjoyed holidays in New York, Egypt, Monte

Carlo and lots of other places. We would walk for hours at a time exploring, something she would never be able to do now. I remember when we were on a Mediterranean cruise for two weeks and we stopped at different places. We would get off and explore and walk or jog around the ship, burning calories and taking in the sun. Mum wasn't one for taking it easy. She looked upon a cruise ship as a giant treadmill on the sea. I had planned to book mum a cruise for her 50th birthday. Those plans have been shelved; a cruise ship isn't the environment for a mobility scooter, something I have discussed with my friend who is an Entertainment Director on P&O Cruises. Another memory that makes me sad as I get older is that I cannot enjoy the simple things like walking around a cruise ship or exploring a new city with my mum. In April 2011, mum and I abseiled down the Europa Hotel, Belfast for the charity FASA. Once again Mum was the first over the top, there was no holding her back and it is something I know my mum will never be able to do again. She was always so active.

Nowadays, mum and I do a bit of light shopping in Abbey Centre. She sets a timer on her phone as she can only walk around for so long before her pain level goes through the roof. She sits down a lot in the few shops that we go into and I'm always conscious of looking for the nearest chair for her to sit in as her pain levels kick in, sometimes very suddenly. I miss taking her to Belfast and being able to walk around the city for hours. The majority of the time I finish my mum's shopping for her while she goes outside and sits in the car or sits on boxes or stools in the shop. Totally the norm for her now. People often look at her if she sits on the stool or boxes and sometimes ask if she's ok. If she didn't sit and manage her chronic pain she would be in agony the rest of the day. It's not unusual that she sometimes resorts to kneeling or sitting on the floor if there are no chairs, stools or boxes nearby.

We enjoyed a holiday to Tenerife in March a few years ago for the first time. We hired a mobility scooter for the full week. My mum used this to get from the hotel down to the seafront, it was no more than a 10 minute walk. In years gone by, we would have walked it no problem, indeed it was part of the fun of getting to the beach. Mum loved the sea and swimming, now walking on sand is almost impossible for her.

We all take simple things like the airport trip for granted. At least we did. Not now. I am more than aware of the long walks to departure lounges – 15/20 minutes are a big *no no*. As soon as we arrive at the airport we have to go to the disability desk and collect a wheelchair. I then push her around the airport which upsets me greatly, especially when people stare because my mum looks so young. It looks like there is nothing wrong with her but if only they knew what she goes through every day of her life.

We've had many people call us lazy and shout things on holiday when we've used a mobility scooter. People have no idea the chronic pain my mum endures on a day to day basis. We would not be able to go to Tenerife if it wasn't for the use of the scooters. I have yet to find another destination that suits us that is not hilly and has use of the mobility scooters and so we head back to Tenerife every year.

I run a successful entertainment business. I believe my mum could have helped me a lot with my business but she can only do so much. She spends most days managing her pain or parking in a disabled bay to walk into a few shops which gets her out of the house.

It upsets me greatly when I see my mum troubled. She gets upset when she sees joggers out running, which is almost every day. I still dance and I have a lot of dancers that work for me. I'm sure this upsets her too as she used to love dancing for hours. She danced from the age of five doing Irish dancing, tap, ballet and Latin American. She was always last to leave the floor. Now, that has been taken away from her.

If we ever go out together, my dad will drop her off at a restaurant and then we get taxis to a few different places as she cannot walk around the city centre. She only stays out for a few hours and I have to make sure that wherever we are going there is a seat available or a table and chair for us to sit at.

I sometimes think of the future and having children and I worry about my mum helping with her grandchildren. This upsets me deeply as I think of going on long walks and pushing a pram with my mum but that will never happen. I try to be there for my mum as best as I possibly can but I have my business to run which can be very demanding at times. I try to visit her four or five times a week and a lot of the time she is upset and frustrated about not being able to get out and be active like before.

It upsets me seeing my mum use her stair lift. It takes 45 seconds every time she goes upstairs to use the bathroom or check on the dogs. Anytime we go out for a family drive, my mum sits in the car and my dad and I go out and walk the dogs. We used to walk the dogs up the country or on the beach and climb up Slemish Mountain every Easter. It's very upsetting as she used to be so active and would always be out walking with us too.

Also, a flashback to last year. I was in total shock at what happened in court in April 2019. I couldn't believe what the lawyers and barristers had done to my parents and neither could my partner Stephen. For many months after I would cry several times a week in the early hours of the morning thinking of the state they had left my poor mum in and the unjust dealings at the court door. My partner Stephen had to lift me off the floor many nights as I was in such a state. They had just left my mum like a dog; no help, no care, nothing. My poor dad was left to pick up the pieces. Once, my mum got the new evidence only two weeks after court, which she passed onto the solicitors. They didn't want to know. It just goes to show they were all about money, greed and lining their own pockets.

I'm very proud of my Mum. She took on the system and fought for all those years for the truth. She always told me, 'Have faith, don't worry, everything's going to be ok, the truth will out.' She's my role model and inspiration, even after everything

she's been through, from her neighbourhood dispute
and now her lifetime injury; she remains strong and
is a fighter.

My Road Ahead

Diane

I have never been in trouble in my life until Denise Black started making up stories. In my mind, there has been a disgraceful abuse of power and a total waste of police time and taxpayers' money.

I have my friend, Marty McGartland to thank as he was the one who suggested starting up my social media page and putting my evidence and story out there. He has been my confidante over the past couple of years. Marty does not mind me making him part of my story, and I believe he is an essential cog in it because if it were not for him I might not be here today. He was there for me when no one else was.

If I could give any advice to you, if you ever find yourself wrongly in the legal system, then it is this: Ensure that you go before a jury. Many people have the impression that judges hate juries - perhaps they take too much of their power away. On the other hand, if you feel as if your barrister and solicitor aren't working for you then represent yourself so that you can ask the correct questions and catch out mistruths in court. I can't help but think, from my experiences that I've noted here, dirty little deals are being done behind closed doors. They certainly seem to have done so with me!

Writing this book has been a healing process, of that there's no doubt. I have felt mentally more in control from the moment I started to scribble the words onto paper. I have been traumatised for the past 13 years and finally, for the first time, I have now been able to get the truth of what happened to me into book form that no one could take away from me. Freedom of speech as a wonderful preserve.

I had previously set up a website and other social